Befriending
Your
Teenager

BEFRIENDING YOUR TEENAGER

How to
Prevent a
Crisis from
Happening

William R. Grimbol

AUGSBURG
Minneapolis

BEFRIENDING YOUR TEENAGER
How to Prevent a Crisis from Happening

Scripture quotations unless otherwise noted are from the Holy Bible: New International Version. Copyright © 1978 by the New York International Bible Society. Used by permission of Zondervan Bible Publishers.

Cover design: Terry Dugan

Library of Congress Cataloging-in-Publication Data

Grimbol, William R., 1949–
    Befriending your teenager : how to prevent a crisis from happening
  / William R. Grimbol.
      p. cm.
    ISBN 0-8066-2550-3.
    1. Parenting—Religious aspects—Christianity. 2. Teenagers—
Religious life. 3. Suicide—Religious aspects—Christianity.
4. Church work with teenagers. I. Title.
    BV4529.G74   1991
    649.125—dc20   91-9990
                                                 CIP

The paper used in this publication meets the minimum requirements of American National Standard for Information Sciences—Permanence of Paper for Printed Library Materials, ANSI Z329.48-1984. ∞™

Manufactured in the U.S.A.   AF 9-2550

95   94   93   92   91   1   2   3   4   5   6   7   8   9   10

To my friends
Hedy and Lenny,
my mom and dad

CONTENTS

PREFACE

Last year I shared a pleasant reunion dinner and conversation with good friends from the congregation I had served in Whitefish Bay, a suburb of Milwaukee, Wisconsin.

Because I had been the pastor to their teenage sons and daughters for eight years, and because they knew of my keen interest in preventing adolescent suicide, it seemed quite natural for the conversation that evening to focus on this topic. Their questions were typical of parents: "How big a problem is it, really?" "What are the warning signs?" "Don't you think that many teenagers just want attention when they talk all this suicide stuff?"

Almost by remote control—owing to the fact that over the past five years I have conducted or facilitated over two hundred workshops, seminars, and retreats on adolescent depression and suicide—I rattled off my answers.

"In the past thirty years, the teen suicide rate has increased over 300 percent, and at the present time one out of every ten American young people will attempt suicide before the age of nineteen. There is a teen suicide attempt in this country every ninety seconds; every day 1,000 of our youth try to take their own lives. This year, 500,000 youth between the ages of fifteen and twenty-four will attempt suicide, and every ninety minutes one of them will succeed.

"Warning signs. Well, you can look for a preoccupation with death or suicide, unexplained crying, or a young person giving away prized possessions. Erratic sleeping habits. Appetite loss. Personality changes. Frequent irritability. Have they lost interest in school or their favorite activities? Do you suspect increased use of drugs or alcohol? Does their behavior appear overly reckless or impulsive?

"Attention? Yes, every suicidal threat, attempt, or success, is a cry for attention. The real issue for us is to realize that whenever an adolescent pleads for attention, no matter how dramatic or self-pitying or even infantile it might seem, we would be wise in today's world to take that plea seriously. We have everything to lose if we don't."

Feeling smug in my mastery of the topic, I suddenly took note of the look in the eyes of these parents and friends. I saw fear and an overwhelming pain. I saw terror. Then, one mother spoke: "Bill, you have to give us more than signs and statistics. Every day we are bombarded with scary stuff about our kids. Anorexia. Drugs. Alcohol. Cults. Depression. The impact of the nuclear age. AIDS. Suicide. Bill, don't just scare us, give us some hope. You are talking about my kid, my little boy, my baby. What can we do? *What can we do?*"

How could I have missed it? How could I have neglected to let myself *feel* that I was talking about their children? I spewed forth teen suicide statistics as if they were the latest economic indicators. These were mothers and fathers, moms and dads, I was speaking to—parents who ache when their teenagers hurt or feel rejected. Parents whose teenagers' tears roll down their own cheeks as well. Parents who get goosebumps when glimpsing from the doorway their kids sound asleep, or when their awkward, self-centered teens give a hug or the world's quickest kiss.

As I looked into the eyes of that small group of friends, I realized something about parents, something I believe I will never again let myself forget, something I know in my heart to be true. *Most* parents are good people, and a vast majority are good parents who would do literally anything to keep their children alive and to enable their adolescents to enter adulthood with enthusiasm and confidence. The parents of teenagers, an oft critiqued, maligned, unaffirmed, ignored, or callously dealt with group of folks (as my own case illustrates), are searching for something beyond statistics and warning signs. They seek a strategy for *preventing* the tragedy of teenage suicide. *They want help to help! They want to do something about it!*

INTRODUCTION

Arriving a few minutes early at the playground, I hoped to catch a glimpse of my five-year-old son Justin's efforts at the art of socialization, and to observe the summer day camp program in which we had him enrolled. It quickly became obvious that at the close of each day, the teachers would hurriedly clean up and then try to relax with a mug of coffee, while the kids had full rein of the swings and slide and sandbox. It was equally apparent from the din emitting from the playground area that this was the day's highlight for the kids. I knew it would be for Justin, who greeted any invitation to play, or any withdrawal of structure, with a passion.

I meandered toward the swing and slide and noticed my son at the foot of the largest slide. I decided to stay at a distance that allowed me to watch undetected. As Justin climbed about midway up the ladder, a chunky child of eight or nine, with a memorable crewcut, grabbed him from behind and lowered him to the sand below. Justin, who had not yet taken this particular socialization course, dusted himself off, stared blankly at the older kid, and proceeded back up the ladder. Once again, the child Neanderthal deposited him on the ground. Justin endured this new and confusing and "unfun" game four times, while his father stood trying to figure out an appropriate response. Upon significant reflection and a momentary appeal for the will of God, I decided to simply *kill* this bully, despite visions of staggering lawsuits lingering in my mind as I strode over to intervene.

I walked up to this miniature Rambo, and told him through a forced grin that he would be wise to allow Justin access to the slide. Still quite oblivious to the ways of the world, Justin sailed down the slide with a loud whoop and, with innocent grace, told the older boy it was his turn. Justin and I then walked hand-in-hand back to our car, he smiling and recounting the day's escapades, and I watery-eyed, still tasting the bitterness of petty injustice.

Driving home that day, I experienced a number of emotions, most notably an empty feeling accompanying my recognition that there would be *few* such opportunities for direct intervention in Justin's life. The simple fact is that Justin's life will be riddled with problems and pain, as all lives are, and a bulk of the time his Daddy will be able to *do nothing about it.* Life will pull Justin to the ground, maybe often, and force him to play unfun games and encounter some nasty folks— folks who will periodically bombard him with unfairness. His life, especially his adolescence, will not be easy, and I can't *do* much to alter that fact. To a devoted Daddy with a desire to protect Justin from the craziness of the world and to control his environment, that is a disheartening acknowledgment.

As is so often the case, however, when we adults are spiritually mature enough to accept our powerlessness, to admit our complete lack of control over a situation, we are then sensitized to God's will. Driving home that day with a son who was not nearly as damaged or defeated as his Dad, I experienced what I choose to call a revelation: Though I might not be able to *do anything* about the course of Justin's life, I can *be someone* who enables him, by spiritual example, to live with the kind of integrity that makes for a genuinely good life. Simply put, I may not be able to *do anything,* but I can *be plenty.*

We can all *be plenty* for our kids, especially for our teen-agers, as we choose in faith to offer real help in the battle with growing pains—a battle that in the modern world resem-bles war, and that is too often just as lethal. We can *be* the kind of adult role models our youth so desperately seek— authentic examples of happy, healthy, honest, and hope-filled lives. We can *be* the "wind beneath their wings," as the refrain of a song declares, the winds of courage and strength and spiritual conviction. We cannot win the battle with growing pains *for* our teenagers, but we can give them inspiration and the taste of victory.

This, then, is not another book dedicated to what to *do* about teenagers, about their problems or their pains, about their pasts or their futures, or even about their values, morals, ethics, or faith. This book is dedicated to *you*—the parent, the pastor, the youth worker, the teacher, the counselor, the coach, the grandparent, the neighbor, the person of faith. This book is dedicated to *being,* to *being* adults whose whole lives reflect a joy in living, a capacity to handle conflict even when life hurls us to the ground, and a commitment to keep learning, growing, and dreaming. This book believes our youth need us to show them more than just how to *make a living;* they need us to show them how to *enjoy a living,* something we cannot *do,* but can choose in faith to *be.*

BE
AWARE

If I were to begin life again, I should
want it as it was. I would only open
my eyes a little more.
                            —Jules Renard

If you have the attitude that adolescents of every era have to go through the same growing pains, or that this generation of youth is just weaker and that is why the teen suicide rate is skyrocketing, consider the following incidents.

Be Aware of the Times

I was stunned a while ago by the reaction of a few youngsters from our youth group to the sudden cancellation of a class trip to Spain. The cancellation was in response to parental outcry following the terrorist bombing of Pan Am flight 103 over Lockerbie, Scotland, a brutal tragedy that claimed the lives of several young students from nearby Syracuse University. Though I expected their bitter disappointment, I did not anticipate their lack of sympathy with their parents' concerns.

As Harry, age seventeen, put it, "Come on, Pastor Bill, we all know we can get blown away any time, any place. You just have to take your chances, that's just the way the world is." I can't even imagine being a teenager in a world that expects one to take such *insane* chances.

Paul, a sixteen-year-old member of my youth group, was particularly down one evening at our Monday discussion group. He seemed in a fog, distant, detached. When he put his head down on the table during the discussion, it was clear something was going on. I requested that he stop by my office after the meeting. When he arrived I simply asked him what was going on. "Pastor Bill," he said quietly, "I took my little brother, Phillip, who's in kindergarten, to be fingerprinted today. My Mom was working, so I had to take him. It's a new program. All the kindergartners went to be fingerprinted. It felt weird. Really weird. I never thought about someone kidnapping him before, but I guess it could happen. It just felt so strange." Yes, strange, weird, indeed.

Last year at a retreat for high school youth, the group struggled to come up with a list of contemporary heroes. The kids howled with laughter when I teased them about wanting to put the pop singer Bon Jovi on a list that at present contained only the names of the president, the pope, and Mother Teresa. For fifteen minutes we tried to come up with ten people who qualified in their minds as heroes, but we remained stuck at the initial three. On a whim, I asked if they could come up with a list of serial murderers. The list was at six in about two minutes flat.

One Halloween they were laughing hysterically, sitting in a circle on the youth center floor. They were so proud. Proud of their creative costuming, especially of Mike's red cardboard box covering him neck to knee, with legs, arms, and face all painted white—a brick. Proud of their trick-or-treating haul, a full shopping bag indicating hours of door knocking. Proud of being teenagers courageous enough to be little kids for one silly night. They sat sorting through their junk food bonanza, searching for hidden razor blades, pins, or needles.

I recall hearing the news that a young man from a university in Texas had been kidnapped while on a partying sojourn to Mexico, and had become the victim of a cultic murder spree. His decapitated body, with brains drained and genitals removed for ritualistic purpose, was discovered on a Mexican farm in a shallow grave that had become a sacrificial altar. I thought about my own son: What if he had been the one? I thought about the kids to whom I minister daily: What if it had been one of them? I thought of this young man's family, and how incomprehensible must be their pain. The whole scenario was absurd, like a teenage horror movie. I felt numb. I still do.

We live in petrifying times, and we adults must *be aware* of the silent terror our adolescents cannot fully express, but that grows deep within their minds. Our youth live under clouds of acid rain, a disintegrating ozone layer, and not just *the* bomb, but millions of bombs and missiles and warheads. The terrorist threat—the terrorist bomb, the terrorist-occupied airliner, the terrorist kidnapping—has become the symbol of our times. We must *be aware* of the quiet erosion of our spirits, teen and adult alike, that is the profound consequence of living in these times. We can nod our heads in understanding the next time we hear someone say, "These kids live like there is no tomorrow!"

Today's teens swing on the trapeze of adolescence, from childhood to adulthood, with nothing but cement pavement far below to catch them if they fall. They fly, pretending in mock sophistication to be unafraid, without a secure perch to push from or a safe place to land. As one young man commented after witnessing the Challenger space shuttle explosion, "Well, now I know *nothing* is really certain." I would

19

guess that all teenagers today have recognized, at some level of their beings, that life comes without warranties, guarantees, or certainties. Maybe life always has been this way, but never before, I believe, has a generation of young people been so ceaselessly bombarded with this fact.

As parents, grandparents, teachers, pastors, counselors, neighbors, or adult Christian friends of adolescents, we must *be aware* of the forces of anxiety pressuring these young lives. In the midst of much plenty stands a generation of youth wanting safety and security, wanting peace of heart and mind. Let us all *be aware* that many of today's teen suicides are linked directly to our adult failure to weave a firm and flexible net—a net of adult faith, courage, and hope—under the acrobatics of our teenagers as they mature.

You may be feeling overwhelmed by so much *bad news.* But if we want to help prevent growing pains from killing our youth, we must admit the fears in our hearts, and *be aware* of the fears in our children's eyes. If we cannot acknowledge this fear, we become adults better suited to life on "The Brady Bunch" than in the real world. If we really want to help, we must examine the contemporary context that contributes to teen suicides.

We explore teen culture with Christ as our guide, and as the guarantee that there is Good News in him. Remember, we are free to the degree we are *aware,* because there are no options, choices, or decisions available to those living unaware in the dark.

Be Aware of False Images

One outstanding component of today's culture is the number of false images our youth often are tempted to copy. A false image is an image that reflects either the desire to be God or the experience of God's absence. Let us review several false images our youth either choose or are coerced to play out in their lives.

The Preppie (or Jock)

One of the most common false images of adolescence today is the preppie, which is a mold crafted of cultural *rightness.* (The jock image carries many of the same characteristics in its own frame of reference.) The preppie must wear the right clothes, know the right people, go to the right schools, earn the right grades and awards, and talk and act from the right preppie perspective. If this sounds like the age-old "in crowd" phenomenon, we must consider the following potentially lethal standards, which prescribe that preppies are:

• *Never vulnerable.* Many youth who desperately pursue preppie status become walking volcanos of hidden hurts and fears, loneliness, anger, or lost love.

• *Never average.* The repugnance many young people feel for being ordinary, common, average, is the direct result of the demand for all preppies to consider themselves extraordinary. The preppie mandate to stand out, stand above, be superior, can be a deadly stress on young lives.

• *Always attractive.* The fixation that so many preppie-oriented teens have on external appearances is costly, not only because of designer tastes but in the creation of eating disorders that result from their obsession with their weight. The preppie mold requires youngsters to be lean and athletic, and some are literally killing themselves to meet the severe standards.

• *Always happy.* The tragedy of teenagers who try to live out this falsehood is that they often pursue at any price pleasures that are supposed to yield happiness. Often the result is excessive partying, casual sex, and the abuse of alcohol and drugs.

• *Cynical.* Sadly, it has become fashionable again to be callous, cold, calculating, clever, and compassionless. The placing of the self on a pedestal is a sad fact of our times. Ignoring or condemning others usually follows.

• *Never kill themselves.* Beyond the standard myth of immortality that serves as the foundation for so many of the preppie fast-lane life-styles, exists the illusion that all preppies are cool, calm, collected, contented souls. The fact is, many of the teen suicides we read about in our local newspapers are youth our culture would brand *preppie.*

If you have chosen to believe that your son or daughter is fine simply because he or she is popular, academically and athletically successful, good looking, sophisticated, or seemingly well-adjusted, it may be time to look again. This is not to say your child is not all of the above, but to remind you that being all-American is no guarantee of teenage happiness. There are too many teenagers out there who have found being a preppie an experience of deadness. They kill their original thoughts. They anesthetize their God-given feelings. They disown their values and their dreams. They sever themselves from the wisdom of the heart. They deaden themselves to the compassionate wishes of their Spirit-inspired spirit. We need to *be aware* of what exists beneath the surface of the preppie image, for only then will we uncover the real truth about our teenagers' emotional, spiritual, and physical health.

Simply put, being a preppie is definitely not as desirable as it is portrayed and can be instead the catalyst for many adolescent crack-ups. If I sound exceptionally harsh toward this adolescent role model, it is because I have witnessed its deadly emphases on conformity, denial of humanness, and its standards and expectations.

The Druggie

Steve is sixteen, an average student, and a nonathlete. He says, "There is nothing really outstanding about me." Steve came to see me after hearing me speak on the subject of teen suicide, something he was struggling with. As he shared his story with me, I was struck by both the tragedy of what he said and by the realization that his experience is commonplace. Let me share Steve's experience with you in his own words, as best I can recall.

"I've never been much good at anything, I mean real good. I get C's, some D's, and a few B's. I was really good in Little League, in baseball, but I was big for my age and now everyone has caught up to me. I was a star when I was ten. Last year I got cut from the junior varsity. I tried going out for the drama club, but I'm pretty shy and I just got so nervous before auditions that I left and went home. I've always wanted to fit in, but I've never found a group where I really fit.

"Last year I decided I'd start dressing weird. You know, lots of leather, lots of black, the punky hair, the whole trip. I went to a couple of parties, got high a couple of times, but it was a total waste. I hated it, but now I'm branded. In two weeks I became a druggie, and they are not about to let me out of that label. No matter how I look now, I'm still the weird kid with the 'punky do.' I'm trapped. I guess killing myself seemed like one way out. Hell, being branded a druggie is killing me anyway."

In our high school corridors walk thousands of teenagers who have been indelibly and inaccurately branded. Within our culture it is unbelievably easy for adolescents to be branded druggies, losers, failures—for reasons that are often beyond their control, for factors that are at best temporary. Adolescents frequently are unfairly branded as losers or burnouts if they:

- are average or below average students;
- are nonathletes;
- are physically unattractive;
- dress unfashionably;
- or cannot afford the "designer competition";

23

- have experimented with drugs;
- have become sexually active at a young age;
- have a parent with a "reputation";
- have befriended the "wrong crowd";
- are politically and socially aware and active;
- are in any way, shape, or form eccentric or original.

The American high school is a notoriously competitive domain, an unforgiving and highly judgmental context. The setting could serve as a visual aid for the opposite of grace. We adults need to *be aware* of how quickly youth are branded, and of how brands are difficult to alter and, frequently, are unfairly applied. For untold numbers of teens, the future looks bleak because of factors they cannot control, mistakes made in the past, or failed attempts to find a niche. We must *be aware* of the deadly seriousness with which adolescents deal with branding, and being branded.

The Nerd

Marie was an honor student; in fact, she had only one grade below an A in her entire high school career: a C in physical education. She was especially talented in science and regularly took first prize at the science fair. She came from a strict, religious home, always dressed in an "old-fashioned" way, and had an admitted tendency to be judgmental of her peers. She was a loner and felt awkward in any social gathering that included young men. She possessed both a sharp tongue and a quick temper prone to inappropriate outbursts. Though Marie projected an image of intellectual and moral superiority, heartily endorsed by her parents, she was noticeably fragile and vulnerable. She called me the night of her senior prom because she was feeling suicidal. The dam had finally burst, and the wall of invulnerability collapsed.

Marie is a female nerd, at least that is how she would be labeled in most of our high schools. Her male equivalent, the not-so-attractive, nonathletic, socially awkward, sometimes academically brilliant, and always unfashionable young man, also called a "geek," has become immortalized in a sad series of movies about the supposed "revenge of the nerds." Ask teenagers to name the nerds in their school and they will come up with a short but brutally well-known list. We must *be aware* of the silent, deadly pain of any adolescent afflicted with such a brand, and of the fact that every Marie will face a senior prom—that night when the volcano of loneliness is likely to erupt. We must *be aware* that such an adolescent will primarily seek revenge not on others, but on him or herself.

Too Good to Be True

Gary was too good to be true. Good looking. Good student. Good athlete. Good musician. Good manners. Good citizen. Good leader at school and within his church youth group. A parent's dream. A teacher's dream. A youth leader's dream. But his life became for him a nightmare of perfectionism, a compulsive quest to always *be good.* He was suicidal when he came to see me.

If there is one adolescent most prone to having occasional suicidal thoughts, or frequently being depressed, it is the teen who can be described as *too good to be true.* Beyond the cultural conformity demanded of the preppie, the adolescent who is too good to be true has added the awesome pressure to be a saint, a status impossible for any adolescent to achieve, and unhealthy for any youth to pursue. Even a preppie wants no part of trying to be a saint.

Adolescence, by its very nature, is often filled with turbulent emotions, sexual confusion, conflicts over gaining independence, and the scrambling search for a true identity. Adolescents who come through this stormy period as though they are in complete control are often adolescents weighed down by the stress of trying to meet everyone's needs and expectations. *Be aware* that the youth who is too good to be true may be attempting to be better than any adolescent should be or could be. *Be aware* that every adolescent needs to admit some insecurity, some awkwardness, some rebellion, and some moral mistakes. The teen who is too good to be true has a long way to fall, and the fall can be fatal.

Be Aware of False Idolatries

Our culture falsely worships three philosophical perspectives on life, and we as adults must *be aware* of their awesome impact on adolescents. Stop and consider how difficult it is for a teenager to enter into adulthood with much genuine energy or excitement in the face of these idolatrous attitudes:

• *You are what you do.* Your worth is always measured by your productivity, and if this productivity is not impressive, your value to society erodes. Such a philosophy creates not only a deep-seated terror of growing old when productivity (on some levels) naturally declines, but also a fear of ever letting down, of being depressed, or of being ill, or grief stricken, or of just doing nothing.

• *You are what you own.* We see the moral bankruptcy of materialism when we become aware that the addiction to the accumulation of possessions can kill off adolescent sensitivity and compassion. So many teenagers ask "Is that all there is?" in the midst of unbelievable opulence and excess. Their lives become shallow and their values self-centered.

• *Stay forever young.* Why would an adolescent want to become an adult when so many adults seem to want to be eternal adolescents? In a nation obsessed with tucking and trimming every ounce of age away, it is little wonder that adolescents approach maturation with some degree of dread.

We must *be aware* that these perspectives negatively affect an adolescent's hope to be a good person, to become a good friend or neighbor or parent, or to try to make a positive difference in the world. This trio of philosophies encourages immaturity, avoidance of intimacy and commitment and responsibility, pursuit of pleasure at all costs, and avoidance or denial of anything or anyone who might make one feel deeply, think seriously, or believe passionately.

BE
HAPPY

*Happiness is the only sanction of
life; where happiness fails, existence
remains a mad lamentable experi-
ment.   —George Santayana*

All I want is for you to be happy." How many times have
teenagers heard their parents or other caring adults echo this
refrain? How many teenagers believe us when we say it? How
many teenagers feel we adults know anything about happiness
in the first place? How many believe that we adults are happy
with our lives? How many of us *are* happy?

"All I want is for you to be happy" would sound a good
deal more convincing if it were spoken by adults who did not
seem so worn out, so highly stressed, so anxious and irritable
much of the time, so angry with the past, so confounded by
the present, and so frightened by the future. Why do we expect
our teenagers to be happy if we don't seem able to master
that goal ourselves?

Where Happiness Fails

My best friend since college days recently paid me a visit. I
invited him to one of the regular youth nights at our youth

center. Since Bob is an amazing storyteller, and adolescents love to hear adult stories—especially if they are true and funny—I knew it would be a grand night for everyone.

Bob held the group captive for nearly an hour, weaving a hysterical tapestry of embarrassing incidents from the college days of Bill Grimbol. The youth ate this up, and I knew these stories would haunt me for some time. To turn the tables, I finally asked him, "Tell the one about your first blind date." The look Bob gave me could have felled a buffalo at one hundred yards, but he knew he had to comply, as the young gathering was already chanting, "Let's hear it!"

Bob told of his ecstasy when a guy he met in homeroom had asked him to double date with his girlfriend's cousin. When that fateful Saturday night arrived Bob scurried to get ready, trying to look and smell perfect. After overcoming the initial awkwardness, Bob started to relax. But with the easing of blind-date tensions came the awareness that he was famished. In his nervousness he had skipped breakfast, skipped lunch in order to get off work early, and was just realizing he had not eaten all day.

At the Dog 'N' Suds Drive-in, Bob ordered enough food to feed Ohio—a fact duly noted by his date. When the food arrived, Bob irritated both his date and the other couple by grabbing for a pouch of onion rings before the carhop had even settled the tray on the window.

After stuffing the last two onion rings in his mouth, Bob started to cough and choke. As the sputtering and hacking continued, he knew something was wrong. To his horror, one particularly volcanic cough brought up a long piece of onion and sent it out through one of his nostrils. My youth group and I erupted in side-splitting laughter. As Bob mimicked his cries of pain as he tried to pull the onion out of his nose, our laughter grew convulsive, uncontrollable. Needless to say, Bob's first blind date made them take her home *immediately.*

As the youth night drew to a close, the group splintered off, some heading home, some staying to chat outside the center, and a few guys hanging back to have a few last words with Bob and myself. One of these young men surprised me by saying, "Pastor Bill, I've never seen you laugh so hard, or be so happy. You should have Bob out more often." The quartet of guys behind him nodded in enthusiastic agreement.

I had never really thought about it until that moment that my youth group had never seen me laugh until the tears rolled. My youth group, to whom I minister daily in an effort to inspire faith, hope, and love, was even uncertain as to whether or not I was genuinely happy, or for that matter, capable of experiencing exuberant happiness. *Of course I am, of course I can,* I thought to myself, but the sad fact remained that they had not witnessed all that much happiness in my life, nor did they recognize me as a happy person.

As adults we often appear to have failed at happiness. We walk through our lives with a shroud of stress over our shoulders, talking to one another as if the goal of life was to stay busy and serious. We wag a finger in the faces of adolescents, telling them of the perils of the real world. We seldom talk to teenagers of anything but grades, drugs, sex, SAT scores, and how the human condition and world are deteriorating at an alarming rate. Oh sure, we try to compensate with an occasional pep talk about how these youths are the hope of the future, or how they can be anything they want to be, but both adolescents and adults fail to believe this tired little speech.

Today's teenager probably does not need to hear any wornout pep talk or any cliche that simplifies the staggering complexity of modern living. What today's teenager needs is to know that becoming an adult is not some bland, bleak experience of boredom, intermittently interrupted by storms of grief or showers of joy. Is it any wonder so many youth question the value of life when we adults make adulthood a rat race, an endurance test of back-breaking, heart-breaking, spirit-breaking difficulty? Think about it. When was the last time your teenager, or the youth you work with and care about, saw *you* really laugh, really look happy? I have come to realize that I owe it to these young people to share openly my happiness; more importantly, the greatest gift I can give them is a happier me. If we want them to choose life, which I know we deeply do, we must make adulthood—the bulk of every lifetime—more appealing, much happier. We do not need to hide our struggles from them, but we do need to let them see our joy, our delight in being alive.

Happiness Cannot Be Bought

I once instructed my confirmation class to write an essay in which they held an imaginary conversation with Christ, surveying all the possessions within their own rooms, and defending to Christ which of those possessions they claimed were necessities. The essay stirred more than a little protest with several confirmands protesting that it was a setup. On the night the essays were due, one young man, Kyle, asked if I had done a similar survey of my own possessions. The class became a Greek chorus, chanting the spirit of Kyle's sentiments and demanding a truthful answer. I agreed to come back the next week with my personal accounting to Christ of what I owned that was necessary, and what Christ would help me classify as luxury.

My survey, my imaginary conversation with Christ, my anticipation of sharing my findings with twenty-four teenagers was, to say the least, disturbing. It was, and still is, unbelievable how much I own, and how little of it deserves the label *necessity.* It was, and still is, humbling to face the lip-service I have paid to the admonitions of the Christ of Scripture:

> Do not store up for yourselves treasures on earth, where moth and rust destroy, and where thieves break in and steal. But store up for yourselves treasure in heaven, where moth and rust do not destroy, and where thieves do not break in and steal. For where your treasure is, there your heart will be also. . . . You cannot serve both God and Money. (Matt. 6:19-21, 24)

> "Watch out! Be on your guard against all kinds of greed; a man's life does not consist in the abundance of his possessions." (Luke 12:15)

How much easier it is to understand the feelings that led to the crucifixion of Christ when we admit to ourselves our addiction to things, possessions, wealth.

The confirmation class arrived the next week eager, delighted in knowing that their pastor would soon confess his shortcomings in the necessity versus luxury debate. I chose to be rigorously honest. I chose not to offer any tired theology about how it is OK to have a ton of things, as long as one does not love them. I know, we all know, that we are part of a culture possessed by possessions, and that to varying degrees we have all fallen victim to the idolatry of things. As I surveyed my own treasure chest, there was simply no denying the presence of idolatry in my own home, my own life. I acknowledged honestly and faithfully what had become obvious—the reality of my sin.

The young confirmands seemed relieved not to hear excuses from me. They deeply appreciated my willingness to share my failings and to call sin a sin. Hearing the raw truth from their spiritual guide transformed this pack of judgmentalists into a gathering of grace. Their expressions, verbal and visual, were of mercy and compassion. We embarked, over the next several weeks, on a debate of sin, idolatry, the awesome difficulty of following Christ in a consumer culture, and the spiritual crucifixion that comes with every attempt to explain to Christ that our myriad luxuries are, in fact, necessary.

There are few times, really, when teenagers are 100 percent ready and willing to hear what we adults have to say. But that night when I shared my sin was such a time. I know those young people fully grasped the spirit of my message, which was that in spite of my own idolatry, I did know in my heart that things *do not make us happy.* I reminded them again, only this time I know they heard, that their lives, and my own, would never be measured by the width of our pocketbooks, the length of our cars, the value of our homes or the extent of our prestige. Of this I am certain, of this I am confident my confirmands understood: *happiness is never bought.*

Spiritual Standards of Success

There is probably not an adolescent or adult presently living in America who could not easily define this society's standards of success. Success is affixed to the pursuit of the good life, and the good life means money and power.

Ironically, there is also probably not an adolescent or adult living in America who would not admit, to some degree, that the fanatic scramble after the good life has yielded some bad results. Bad feelings. Bad moods. Bad attitudes. Bad faith. Bad marriages. Bad parenting. Bad families. Certainly, bad life-styles.

Even more ironic is that a vast majority of adult Americans would eagerly concur with Ralph Waldo Emerson's definition of success as not only more accurate, more worthy of pursuit, but as capable of yielding a good deal more happiness.

To laugh often and love much; to win the respect of intelligent persons and the affection of children; to earn the approbation of honest critics and to endure the betrayal of false friends; to appreciate beauty; to find the best in others; to give of one's self; to leave the world a bit better, whether by a healthy child, a garden patch, or a redeemed social condition; to have played and laughed with enthusiasm and sung with exultation; to know that even one life has breathed easier because you have lived—this is to have succeeded. (Ralph Waldo Emerson)

As adult Christians it is time for us to wholeheartedly endorse standards of success that yield goodness—good feelings, good friendships and families, good faith, and, indeed, a good deal of happiness. It is time for us to advocate to our adolescents standards of success that are spiritually rooted: attitudes, experiences, behaviors, and beliefs that will bring some happiness to our lives and theirs, happiness that is indeed "the only sanction of life."

"All I want is for you to be happy." To teens with many problems, adolescents struggling to survive, these words only echo emptiness. Suicidal teens, so often wise beyond their years, sensitive beyond their capacity to cope, will reject the notion of a cheaply purchased happiness as the solution to life. Suicidal teens search for a more costly, more satisfying happiness, a happiness with roots in values, morals, relationships, meaning, and real worth. Suicidal teens will gravitate, out of some divine survival instinct, to those adults with smiles and scars, to those adults who, like Emerson, speak the truth as to what really matters, what really lasts.

BE
HUMAN

*The essence of being human is that
one does not seek perfection.*
                              —George Orwell

A friend from college related the following regarding an
incident that occurred while he was in high school in Boston.

The outrageous conduct of Mrs. Carbone, the school
librarian, during fire drills had become a school joke. An
elderly woman of hefty dimensions, with a voice that could
shatter diamonds, Mrs. Carbone would stand at the top of the
library steps clapping her hands loudly, and yelling with drill
sergeant precision, "March! March! March!" Not to have experienced Mrs. Carbone during a fire drill was to have missed
out on a guaranteed high school highlight, an event recalled
well beyond graduation.

One day during a senior study hall, a faint smell of smoke
wafted into the library, and a sniffing Mrs. Carbone began to
pace at the top of the steps. When the fire alarm went off,
she sprang into action, but this time a library full of seniors

anxiously and gratefully awaited her direction. Suddenly a huge puff of thick black smoke burst through an air vent near the library doors, and Mrs. Carbone screamed, "Fire! Everyone get the hell out of here!" She streaked out the door as her "troops" watched in stunned silence. Finally coming to their senses, the bewildered seniors ran out after their leader.

The fire turned out to be four dozen blazing blueberry muffins left unattended in an oven by four freshman boys, who had stepped into the school courtyard to flirt with four freshman girls. Needless to say, Mrs. Carbone's fame hit new heights and even spread to other high schools, to churches, restaurants, department and drug stores, buses and car pools, and most dining room tables within a twenty-mile radius. The seniors wore "Fire! Everyone get the hell out of here!" T-shirts for the remainder of the school year. To this day, it is said, Mrs. Carbone blazes crimson at any mention of that infamous fire drill.

Like Mrs. Carbone, every one of us has had an embarrassing experience that revealed our humanness, an event that exploded the myth of our control, our invulnerability. We need to share these events with adolescents so that we become more human in their eyes. Then, when an explosion rips apart their own illusion of control, as it will, they will be less likely to be devastated. Today's teenagers often lack the coping capacity needed to survive such a crisis and can easily be overwhelmed by any such humiliating experience. At least, if they know that we have survived, that we too have known our crimson moments of mortifying humanness, then we have offered them a symbol of hope. By acknowledging our humanness, an undeniable reality of adulthood, we have borne witness to a basic truth of life, something every teenager must endure. We may hope, however, that when we share our sagas of human frailty and failing, they won't create T-shirts in honor of the event!

The Perfection of Imperfection

It is the will of God for humans to be human. It seems to be the will of humans to resist receiving this gift of humanness. Most adults spend a lifetime trying to be anything but human. Most of us secretly, or not so secretly, want to be in control, in charge, to have conquered life. We tend to treat most signs of humanness as blemishes to be removed, as the foreshadowing of a plunge into "loser" status. Many of us are so obsessed with creating the perfect image, the illusion of the perfect family, the impression of being perfectly together, that even when we say, "I'm only human!" nobody, especially adolescents, believes we mean it.

Many of the youth with whom I work are equally obsessed with such perfectionist images, illusions, and impressions. A majority of the teenagers I have counseled for suicidal thoughts or tendencies are legitimately labeled *perfectionists*. This quest for perfection often expresses itself in various combinations of the following:

- Intolerance of mistakes
- Intolerance of failures
- Intolerance for being just average
- Overreaction to criticism
- Difficulty with boundaries, borders, and limits
- Difficulty with authority figures
- Excessive patronizing of authority figures
- Inability to slow down or, at times, to sleep
- Inability to play
- Inability to do nothing
- Anxiety about prayer or meditation
- Anxiety about any form of spiritual surrender
- Discomfort with worship
- Excessively "saintly" behavior
- Excessive rage when things don't run smoothly

- Excessive rage when things don't go "my way"

The price our teenagers pay for refusing to celebrate being human is often high; at times, tragically, it costs their lives.

As adults we must teach our youth how to acknowledge, affirm, even celebrate *being human.* We must remind them that life was never meant to be smooth or easy. Every teenager has seen a heart monitor on TV or in an actual hospital room. Every teenager knows what a flat smooth line on a heart monitor means. Life *must have* ups and downs, periods of fluctuation, even pronounced ones, as well as times of rolling waves of calm.

We only become aware of the gift of God's grace, the gift of unconditional love and forgiveness, when we have been on our knees long enough to know we are *not* God. The only preparation required to become aware of grace is to walk *humbly* with our God. Humility is not natural for a teenager, and in our achievement-obsessed era, it appears to be culturally out of style as well. If, however, we want our young people to survive their growing pains in modern America, we would be wise to teach them humility, the power of being on one's knees, and the grace that comes from spiritual surrender to our loving God.

Blessed Be the Tie that Binds

The table was meticulously set—the color theme mauve and pale blue, carried out in flowers, napkins, table cloth, and china. All three teenage children were equally spotless, as polished in their table manners as the silver. The father looked regal, water goblet in hand, as he orchestrated both conversation and the distribution of food. The mother sat across from her husband, the essence of serenity, except for a tiara of perspiration on her brow.

My entire pastoral visit to this family had been flawlessly arranged and executed. It was clear, however, that the gathering had grown stiff with awkwardness, tense with the hope of fulfilling Mother's wish for a perfect dinner and evening for the new youth minister. Just as clearly, the impression this precision-like event was supposed to leave with me was that there were "no problems here."

As Father passed the platter of roast beef he had just carved, he failed to consider the tidal movements of the au jus. With one large, pinkish-brown wave, the au jus leaped and splashed its way across the table. Mother, oblivious to anything but the demolition of her perfect dinner, stood and shouted, "Oh (expletive deleted), Henry, nice job!" The kids almost burst from trying to restrain enormous giggles, when Henry gave the cue that laughter was OK. Patting his drooping wife affectionately on the behind, he said, "Well, Betty, I just wanted to make the pastor feel at home."

For the first time that night I felt at home. For the first time the conversation was no longer stilted, but became spontaneous, filled with warmth and laughter. Betty, no longer trapped into being the perfect mother, became a most charming hostess, filling the evening with listening and love. Henry reveled in his new freedom and continued to display obvious affection for his wife, and increased his children's feelings for him when tears came as he described how proud he was of all three. The children, up to this point rather silent, became willing participants in the conversation. As Betty remarked, "I've never heard you three talk so much." I was confident the three adolescents had figured out it was highly unlikely they could top Mom's swearing in front of the minister on his first visit, so they could be themselves.

I have found it to be true that whenever we choose to share our humanness, or our humanity is simply revealed, the potential for genuine intimacy and community is created.

David, a soft-spoken, gentle young man, unwittingly transformed our youth group into a family one evening. Soon to graduate, he risked sharing his deep feelings about that meeting being his final one. In a voice choked with emotion and with a depth I doubt the group believed Dave possessed, he simply said, "Don't wish it away, any of it, not high school, not the youth group, not any of it. Just *don't* wish it away!" Dave's risk, his revelation, altered that evening's youth gathering, freeing us all to display some affection, to acknowledge the importance of one another and the group, and to spontaneously become a true community.

A high school teacher once shared with me that she decided to tell her junior and senior level English classes that she was cranky one day, had a splitting headache, and was just simply not up for a day of teaching. To her surprise, her students responded with respect, compassion, and exemplary behavior. Several stopped in after school to find out if she was doing any better. When she informed her students that they were *not responsible* for her bad day, they responded by trying to make it as good a day as possible.

The need in our culture, in our times, for community and intimacy is both enormous and obvious. This need within our teenagers is critical, and if not addressed can easily become life threatening. As adults, we owe it to our youth to risk sharing and displaying our own humanness, as well as encouraging them to embrace their own. We must cultivate within our teenagers a spiritual awareness that much of what we try to keep *private* is also what we have in *common* with others. Only in sharing our common humanity, our imperfections, will we create community and become both lovable and capable of real intimacy.

When we gather to celebrate the Lord's Supper, we come in a spirit of community, of communion with one another and with God; we come in a spirit of loving our neighbor as our-selves, and our God with our whole heart. We gather at the Lord's table, knowing we have sinned against Christ in thought, word, and deed, relying fully on his grace as the means of regaining our spiritual integrity. As Christians, we have a legacy filled with symbols celebrating things the world chooses to deny or ignore. We know why we call Good Friday *good.* We possess the wisdom to worship a powerless baby in a manger. We know in our hearts that "all things are literally better, lovelier, and more beloved for the imperfections which have been divinely appointed" (John Ruskin, *The Stones of Venice*).

We must offer this sacramental context of safety, protec-tion, and above all else, grace to the troubled or suicidal teenager. In an atmosphere rich with unconditional love, in an environment that embraces all questions, doubts, fears, and mistakes, and that accepts rage, pain, and despair, a troubled teen can begin to heal.

As Christian adults we must "run down the road" to meet any teen we even suspect of contemplating suicide. We must come running when we believe any youth is stooping to eat the food of swine (see Luke 15:11-32). We must come running even before we witness any desire in adolescents to return, to come home, to come to themselves. We must come running, not wagging a finger of judgment, but with arms flung wide with full acceptance, arms prepared to hug the pain away, arms ready to lift up that teenager in a celebration of shared humanness.

BE REAL

It is only with the heart that one can see rightly; what is essential is invisible to the eye.
—Antoine de Saint-Exupery

Our youth group had planned to lead a worship service at a nearby nursing home, but when we arrived we faced disaster. I had dragged twenty-six teenagers through the nursing home doors, only to find that the director of the home had forgotten about us, but now wondered if we would mind conducting the service while the residents ate their lunch. The dismal alternative of amusing my disgruntled herd for another hour or so convinced me to go ahead with our worship service, even if it smacked of a dinner theatre experience.

The group sang the opening hymn, "Day by Day," with lukewarm enthusiasm, as the clanging trays and glasses easily drowned out their feeble efforts. I had given one of my youth the wrong scripture to read. Fortunately, he and this eating throng of elders seemed oblivious to the irony of a passage from Paul about adultery and fornication. Except for our church organist, who couldn't look at me for fear of exploding into laughter, I doubt if anyone heard one word of the Word. Thank God!

The three teen preachers plodded through the same sermon they had delivered with gusto the week before to the entire congregation. The diners were into the tapioca pudding by then, so it was hard to compete with the scraping of bowls. When the worship service wound down with the closing hymn, "Amazing Grace," it was indeed the sweetest sound I'd heard for a long time.

After a brief, rather stormy, debate with them, I strong-armed my youth into taking some time to visit with the residents. We would meet, then, in a half hour (what my group contended was equivalent to eternity) in the parking lot, and return to the church to share our experiences. This last suggestion brought chuckles from my group of cynics; they figured it would take approximately thirty seconds to share our collective significant memories.

In fact, it took almost three hours to "unpack" all that the youth group experienced in their one-on-one encounters. This lengthy period of sharing was both redeeming, the nursing home journey no longer being "a waste," and revealing, in that our youth discovered that these old folks were actually *real human beings.* Listening to the nursing home residents share their loneliness, their joy, their memories, their stories, their wisdom, their questions, their faith, their fury with God, their love, their need to be loved, and their desire to know everything about these youngsters, my group found the oldsters transformed into *real people.* When they experienced what these senior citizens *felt* about everything from life to God to the state of the nation, the issues of their age and condition evaporated and the unique reality of their God-given individuality emerged.

Becoming Real

I could know a good deal about you, what you do during a day, how many children you have, whether you are married, where you are from, what your hobbies are, what kind of car you drive, or even where you like to vacation, but I won't feel like I *know* you until I know what you feel. You will not become *real* for me until I know what makes you laugh or cry, what gives you goosebumps, what hurts your feelings, or what gets your dander up. Only when I feel in touch with your needs, your wishes, your dreams, that whole intricate emotional network, can I honestly say I *know* you, or that you have *become real* to me as a person.

Adolescents as a whole are hungry to know adults as *real people,* as people who can be funny, sad, lonely, or ecstatic. Too often we appear nothing more than robots, sophisticated drudges cranking out life without cracking a smile, shedding a tear, or batting an eye. Many adolescents are desperate to discover our *hearts,* to know what makes us tick, so they can claim us as real people, real friends.

We need to help our adolescents gain an appreciation for the emotional realm, and a deep understanding that adulthood does not eliminate emotion. We need to share with teenagers that life, especially as an adult, is filled with anger, hurt, jealousy, lust, goosebumps, tears, fear, dreams, and hopes, and that we would want it no other way.

Parents frequently ask if it isn't dangerous to share the whole spectrum of adult emotions with adolescents. The opposite is usually the case: most teenagers not only are helped when adults share their feelings, but they often breathe sighs of relief. It is a relief to be released from the heavy weight of acting cool, calm, and collected. It is refreshing to uncover all those powerful, sometimes uncontrollable, vulnerability-revealing emotions.

The following is an account of a teenager's poignant encounter with his father's real feelings. It illustrates both how the teen saw his father transformed from *robot* to *real* through an honest emotional exchange and the healthy effects when an adult shares genuine feelings.

> At first I was stunned. I had never really seen him cry before. I know it was his father's funeral, but I still expected him to be as solid as a rock—like usual. I felt guilty staring at him, but in a way it felt so good to see him cry, do you know what I mean?
>
> I walked up to him after the service, and I knew we both felt weird, but we hugged, and I told him I loved him, and he kept on crying. I never felt so close to him. It made me feel like a man to hold him, I mean to be the one *giving* the hug. It also felt, well, good to know that crying was all right.
>
> My whole relationship to him changed that day. I had never thought of him as a friend, but that day I did. I still do. The best part was that he told me all kinds of stories about Grandpa on the way home from the cemetery, stories I never heard before. Man-to-man stories. That kind of stuff.
>
> Pastor Bill, when I told him that I didn't know he cared so deeply about Grandpa, do you know what my Dad said? He said, "Just imagine what I feel about you, son. Just imagine."
>
> It is kind of sick to say this, but that funeral was one of the best days of my life.

Real tears. Real hugs. Real love. Real friends. Imagine how many teens ache for such an encounter with a parent, an adult who really cares—just imagine.

Although such sharing can become excessive, an unhealthy dependence, or an unreasonable expectation for an adolescent response, I find that to be the exception and not the norm. The positive benefits of careful, cautious sharing of adult emotions with teenagers are many. Adolescents often acquire: confidence in their ability to survive the stresses of maturation, empathy for others, courage to live more authentically, capacity to communicate feelings (so obviously critical to intimacy), and firmer faith (trust in God's wisdom in creating us as such emotional creatures).

God's Vocabulary

I have, at times, speculated that before the arrival of Christ all we knew of God was what God "thought," the external rules and regulations that give life a sense of order. With the event of Jesus the Christ, we finally have come to know the "heart" of God, the essence that infuses life with passion and meaning. Jesus forever destroys the image of a detached, indifferent, even cold and calculating God. The weeping (Luke 19:41-44), angry (Matt. 21:12-13), exuberant (Matt. 11:25-26), and even despairing (Mark 15:34) Jesus, demonstrates the divine personality present in the incarnation.

God seems to speak most loudly through the megaphone of our emotions. We must convey to our youth that the heart bursting with joy, heavy with sorrow, breaking with pain, calloused by anxiety, numbed by loneliness, most clearly tells us God's will and wishes for our lives. It is impossible to ignore messages from the heart, messages carefully written by the Spirit in the language of emotions, messages that reflect God's Word. The truth of our feelings tells us of our need to love and be loved, be respected, be understood, face conflict, make changes, know when to confront or walk away, to speak or to be still. Every adolescent must realize that while we may experience emotions as either bad or good, we deny or ignore them at our peril. Emotions are part of God's vocabulary, one of God's main ways of communication, of getting our attention, of poking us into growth, prodding us into submission, or bringing us back to life.

A Sample Menu

Let me suggest a sample menu of emotions we know are present in various degrees in every adult, emotions adolescents must learn to accept as part of life if they are to become healthy adults. This list could serve as a guide to emotional sharing, a catalyst for good conversation between adults and adolescents, and a reminder to us all to *be real.*

• *Joy.* What still takes your breath away? What makes your eyes twinkle, your stomach flutter, your heart leap? What still gives you goosebumps? When was the last time you thought you would burst with the exuberance of simply being alive?

• *Despair.* When was the last time you felt hopeless? helpless? deserted? When was the last time you felt there was nothing new under the sun? When was the last time your heavy heart seemed to say, "What's the use?"

• *Love.* You were created to love and be loved by God who is love. Where have you found love, even a little? Whom do you love, even a little? How can your love grow?

• *Fear.* Well, what is it: rats, mice, snakes, spiders, heights, depths, dark, water, flying? Or is it death, aging, illness, loss, nuclear bombs, random violence? What about living, loving, learning? They can be scary, too.

• *Need.* Do you accept your need to be needed? Do you admit to needing friends? Do you share your need to speak openly, talk honestly, communicate deeply? Do you need to be understood? respected? trusted? loved? Do you need to be affirmed? acknowledged? shown attention? How?

• *Anger.* When, where, why, with whom? What other emotions are behind it? Fear? Lack of love? Sadness?

• *Jealousy.* You wish you had what the other person has, or you are afraid the other person will get what you have or want. What is behind jealousy? Insecurity? Fear?

- *Shame.* You feel that you aren't good enough, that what you are and do are flawed. How does self-acceptance fit in, or forgiveness?
- *Loneliness.* It can happen in a crowd, in a marriage, in a family. Sometimes you feel that no one really accepts you. How can you overcome loneliness?
- *Grief and sadness.* The losses and defeats in life leave scars, and yet life asks you to live with those scars. Some healing is possible, however. What has helped you?
- *Lust.* It strikes us like a sneeze out of nowhere, and you're caught without warning. What can you do?
- *Courage.* When did you last take a risk? When was the last time God dared you to do something, and you did it?

Depressed teens have lost their appetite for uplifting emotions and suicidal adolescents feel only the heaviest ones. Still, the hunger for missing emotions remains—the hunger to feel, to enjoy, to love, to belong, to hope, to possess energy, to be alive.

It is our responsibility as Christian adults who care about these troubled teens to invite them back to the banquet and encourage them to sample many emotions. Finding a balance is a key to emotional health. In good parental style, we must do all we can to nurse the troubled adolescent back to health, including seeking professional help when that seems wise.

BE
HONEST

*The most important thing in acting is
honesty. If you can fake that, you've
got it made.*   —*George Burns*

We once traveled out to Elmira, New York, where my father
had just completed training for repairing electric typewriters.
His landlady during his schooling had told him to bring his
family out sometime. Three months later we were on our way.

Dad drove and I was his official copilot—so designated
in order to keep my seven-year-old mind and mouth occupied
for the thousand-mile trek. Around the Chicago area, I noted
something curious. Fulfilling my task of reading all signs, I
mentioned to the pilot that this was the third time, I was pretty
darn sure, that I had observed a particular billboard, "Mayor
Daley Welcomes *you* to Chicago," done in enormous red and
blue block letters on a white background.

I was still mentally wrestling with the accuracy of my
observations, when good old Mayor Daley welcomed us for
the fourth time. At this point, Mom began to huff and puff,

49

twist and turn, a maneuver used to signal either a desperate need to go to the bathroom or her suspicion that we were hopelessly lost. When Mayor Daley welcomed us for the fifth time, I knew that all huffs, puffs, twists, and turns symbolized our status as wanderers in the desert, and that we might indeed roam for a good forty years.

"For God's sake, Lenny, just pull into some gas station and ask for directions."

"I know exactly where I went wrong. I've driven for twenty-seven years, you know."

"Well, if Mayor Daley welcomes us for a sixth time, you can just turn this car right around and head home. I'm not driving all the way to New York with someone who can't even admit when he's lost."

My mother's voice sounded confident, because she was sure that Mayor Daley loomed over the horizon. Dad was secretly convinced round six was on its way as well, and so pulled into a Shell station. "Have it your way, Hedy, he'll just tell me what I already know."

In the years since our Elmira journey, I have often wondered why it is so difficult for adults to admit the truth. Why couldn't my father just admit we were lost? Why do I, now that I am an adult, a husband, a father, have such a tough time admitting when I'm lost, especially when wandering in an emotional or spiritual desert? Why do we adults feel so compelled to have the answers and seldom seem willing or able to acknowledge the depth of our questioning?

Sadly, I have witnessed the erosion of adolescent confidence in hearing the truth from adults. Most teenagers expect the truth to be either manipulated for convenience's sake, altered for security's sake, or fabricated for safety's sake. The moral message our youth have received from the Iran-Contra affair, the sexual escapades of TV evangelists, the "don't do drugs" TV ads done by sports heroes who do drugs, the airlines that fail to inform us of terrorist threats, the exposure to product after product that "possibly" causes cancer, is that honesty seldom, if ever, is the best policy.

We see before us a generation of young men and women who fulfill Oscar Wilde's definition of a cynic: someone who knows the price of everything and the value of nothing. We adults seem to be unable to teach today's teens the value of honesty. So many of us have become what Andre Gide defined as the true hypocrite: "the one who ceases to perceive his deception, the one who lies with sincerity." Are we living a lie? Are we true to ourselves? to others? to God? Are we honest emotionally? spiritually?

Adolescents yearn to find adults who speak the truth, act the truth, and conform themselves *honestly* to what they believe their heart and their faith "call" them to be. The only antidote to adolescent cynicism I have ever known to work is adult integrity, and its core is a rigorous honesty.

Living a Lie

There is something basically dishonest in living by an inflexible schedule, in measuring oneself on a yardstick of busyness, or in viewing life as something to plow through. We live a lie when we make living an endurance test, a rat race, an experience we can only handle by becoming detached, indifferent, almost catatonic. Is this not what adolescents often see in the adult world: adults always on the move (but without direction), adults always claiming progress (but displaying no vision), adults always saying they are fine (but looking ragged)? Is it not fair for our teenagers to expect some honest answers from adults, to know where we are going and why, and to find out if we believe it is worth the price of travel?

This section is a direct product of what I am presently experiencing. Let me explain.

I am on a solo writing sojourn to Amherst, Massachusetts, for one full week of solitude, silence, and, of course, writing. I chose Amherst because I love the feel of the town, which, like a grandma's attic, is cluttered with history, memories, stories, and the wonderful aroma of life cherished, of things held sacred.

I have spent my time here taking long walks down streets lined with enormous trees, reading novels in a cozy and Spartanly simple room, eating my meals accompanied by the beauty of the Quabbin reservoir, and indulging myself in long stretches of writing or meditative thought. The net effect is like showering away the dirt acquired while working diligently in the garden. What has awakened in me here in Amherst is a spirit that had been deadened by too much living on automatic pilot. Having been enslaved to a schedule my own pride had created, I find the freedom of wandering in my chosen wilderness spiritually exhilarating. The heart can tingle, quiver, rejoice, if we give it the space, the time, the stillness, the access to the Holy Spirit.

Amherst has jarred me loose; my rigid drive to be the perfect pastor, husband, daddy, friend, person, has given way to an avalanche of spiritual insights, most old (but worthy of repetition), a few brand new. I share this list, which is helping to keep me honest, in an effort to help keep *you* honest:

- Enjoy silence. In silence we begin to hear our callings and God's Spirit. We see more clearly who we are.
- Take a walk. A walk has no destination but return, and symbolically enables us to return to ourselves and our God.
- Be renewed in solitude; it gives a special poignancy to your relationships. Make friends with yourself.
- Slow down. There is no vision in a blizzard of activity.

- Read some good novels. Get to know characters who make you wince or wish you knew them; inhabit a novel's world.
- Have "shrines of beauty." These are places that guarantee beauty, where you can feel awe on a regular basis.
- Invite the questions in for a visit. Become a good host to life's instinctual inquiries: Who am I? Where am I going? What do I wish to be remembered for? What matters? Why bother? Why not? Why?
- Overhear other people's conversations. Remind yourself of how funny and sad, candid and concerned, warm and wonderful people are.
- Evaluate your friendships. Vow to make one major change and a sprinkling of minor ones.
- Let God get to know you.
- Watch a TV show or movie that makes you laugh.
- Open yourself to feelings. Become reacquainted with your griefs, your joys, your needs, and your wishes.
- Dream. Daydream. Fantasize.
- Talk to yourself. Sing to yourself. Whistle.
- Compose lists of letters you want to write; gifts you want to give; places you want to see; things you want to learn; projects you want to complete; and goals you want to work toward. Throw the lists away. Live the lists.
- Do a stewardship review. How are you taking care of your needs? the needs of others? the needs of God?
- Let memories haunt you. Let yourself ache; the Holy Spirit is stretching some atrophied spiritual muscles.
- Laugh or cry.
- Listen.
- Don't take yourself too seriously.

Every adolescent deserves to know one adult who is not living a lie, who is true to self, to God, to the truth. Every adolescent deserves to know one adult who still believes that to love is one's highest calling, and that laughter is a significant achievement. Every adolescent deserves to know one adult who makes lists not of what to *do* today, but what to *be,* and who vows today to be happy or sad, and finds both worthy. Every adolescent deserves to know one adult who still skips, makes angels in the snow, tries to catch raindrops on the tongue, and builds sandcastles, snowmen, and tree forts. I believe that *most* suicidal teenagers have never been friends with such an adult. We can *be that one!*

Lost and Found

Patrick, a college student with whom I had worked while he was in high school, stopped by over a spring break to touch base. It was apparent from his description of his junior year that he was unsettled, dissatisfied, and feeling the urge to be anywhere but in school. In typical pastoral style, I asked him what he was feeling about his present situation, simply to confirm what I already suspected. The following conversation ensued, a conversation I still find fascinating and ironic. It is similar to conversations I have had with several college students.

"I feel a need to travel, Pastor Bill, to just wander for awhile on my own so that I can find myself."

"How did you get lost?"

"What?"

"If you have to be found, you also had to have gotten lost."

"I've never thought about it that way before."

"Well, it would seem to me, Patrick, that before you go looking for yourself, you should make a list of all the places you may have misplaced you."

"Like looking for a wallet?"

"Well, if something feels like it is missing, something has been misplaced. It makes sense to first ask what that something might be, and then where it might be found."

"I just thought the time away would be good for me."

"It probably will be, Patrick, but there are no geographic solutions to life's frustrations, anxieties, boredom."

"Do you think I'll find me?"

"I think you'll find out you've been found from day one, or at least I hope you will."

Our relationship to Christ is often like Patrick's experience of feeling lost, that is, we didn't know we were *getting* lost until we realized we *were* lost. We don't mean to wander away from Christ. We don't mean to live a lie. We don't mean to make life-style choices that deaden our souls, kill our spirits, and sap our energy and enthusiasm. We don't mean to be so dishonest about what we feel, think, believe, want, or need. We don't mean to, but we do.

> I do not understand what I do. For what I want to do I do not do, but what I hate I do. And if I do what I do not want to do, I agree that the law is good. As it is, it is no longer I myself who do it, but it is sin living in me. I know that nothing good lives in me, that is, in my sinful nature. For I have the desire to do what is good, but I cannot carry it out. For what I do is not the good I want to do; no, the evil I do not want to do—this I keep on doing. Now if I do what I do not want to do, it is no longer I who do it, but it is sin living in me that does it. . . . Who will rescue me from this body of death? Thanks be to God—through Jesus Christ our Lord! (Rom. 7:15-20, 24-25)

Maybe the key to honesty lies in acknowledging how frequently we let ourselves get lost, how often we choose to remain hidden, even from our own selves. Maybe the beginning of all honesty is to call out, "God, where are you?" and hear God answer, "Where are *you?*" Maybe we need to let the suicidal teen, or any teen in emotional trouble, know how easy it is to get lost, how natural it is to wander away from our spiritual roots, and how vital it is to scream out when we are lost so that somebody might hear our cry. We need to be honest enough to know that God did not lose us, but we lost track of God—and in so doing seemed to lose ourselves.

BE HEALTHY

Sickness is felt, but health not at all.
—Thomas Fuller, M.D.

I felt a strange anxiety as I drove to the airport. My head throbbed and felt like a fully-blown balloon about to pop. My whole body felt distressed and my feet felt as if they were being tugged down an invisible drain. I worked to keep myself calm, hoping not to snap at my son, who was playing nicely in the backseat.

To some extent this anxiety could have been predicted because I was on my way to pick up my wife, Chris, who was returning from a month-long stay in a food-addiction program near Atlanta. Though I had spoken with her frequently and Chris considered the program not only effective, but transforming, I was still overwhelmed with a strange wonder, as if I were meeting her on a blind date of sorts. I could tell on the phone that my wife was, in many profound ways, a new person, a person who talked freely and firmly about her disease. Chris was convinced that her addiction to food was consuming her life, devouring her spirit, and destroying her health. She had also informed me that she considered herself an alcoholic as well, something I found hard to understand, since Chris drank far less than I. She defended her declaration with these simple, straightforward words, "I know in my heart that even if I deal with my eating, but let myself drink, in a very short time the drinking will replace the food as my primary addiction." I cannot say this all made sense to me, but I was wise enough to know not to tamper with *any* of Chris's choices regarding her health.

My anxiety built and my son's excitement grew as we waited at the gate, holding hands, for her to emerge from her flight. Justin spotted her first, as his excited hopping and shrieking clearly indicated. When my eyes fixed on her familiar frame, I felt all the tension rush out of me, like rain water racing for a sewer after a summer thunderstorm.

In that moment, when peace did pass all understanding, when love for wife and son could have scorched the sun, I made some choices. I weighed 257 pounds. I drank daily. My blood pressure had developed a pattern of unhealthy peaks and valleys. I had tried to control my weight and my drinking for several years, but all efforts to look and feel good had failed. I had been juggling overeating, overdrinking, overworrying, overworking for as long as I could remember, and in some tragically ironic way, had avoided seeking help with my compulsions because I couldn't decide which one to choose. I had an addiction (in fact several) and for the first time in my life the word etched itself on my heart and brain, and would soon come easily off my tongue. My wife's courageous decision to seek help had come home to me, and now inspired my own spiritual awareness. We *both* had a disease called addiction.

Practice What You Preach

My recovery began a couple years ago; since that time Chris and I have continued to seek help in a number of ways. We attend meetings of Alcoholics Anonymous (A.A.) and Over-eaters Anonymous (O.A.). We are in therapy. We try to work the Twelve Steps, applying those principles to other addictions, not just alcohol. We do our best to exercise, meditate, pray, spend ample time with healthy people, and considerable time learning to take good care of ourselves.

I have chosen to share my addictions with my youth group and, when appropriate, within the framework of the workshops I conduct. I do so only because I feel it is so critical for the young people I work with to see me as a *real, honest, human being,* and because I believe addiction is not only epidemic within this country, but in many ways out of control among our adolescents. I no longer find it reassuring when I hear adults say, "I drank that way when I was a teenager, everybody did." Maybe we all did, and maybe we need to admit how many of us never stopped, even when we wanted to.

I have been fascinated, and deeply moved, by the reaction of my youth group to the revelation of my addictions. They consistently affirm me for my weight loss, which is fifty-eight pounds to date, and for the fact that I can now play basketball during the lunch break at school without my face looking like a maraschino cherry. It has been sobering to realize how many of these young kids were secretly worried about my health and my life. I certainly felt some healthy embarrassment when I was told, while sharing a dinner out with a few of these young folks, how good it was to see me not have two or three glasses of wine with my meal. As one of the young men boldly said to me, "It is hard enough to make these choices as it is, it just made it that much harder when we saw you doing the same stuff you encouraged us not to."

It seems almost absurd at this point, to realize that I never recognized fully the importance of practicing what I preach. When I think back on how many times I warned these young people about the possibility of becoming addicts, or how often I heard them tell disturbing stories of living with an addicted parent or sibling, or of dealing with an addicted friend, I never cease to be amazed at the dynamic of denial inherent in this disease, or the extent of my own denial before getting help. I will also never fully lose the joy I feel inside knowing that I am now trying, with the help of God, A.A., O.A., and many other healing addicts, to practice what I preach.

Dis-Ease

Disease. Dis-ease. Out of ease. Out of ease with self. Out of ease with life. Out of ease with God. Out of balance. Out of focus. Out of perspective. Out of it.

The choices I make in regard to life-style either promote health or enable disease. I may not actually create the disease, but I can create the climate, the context conducive to its development. I simply cannot continue to see health as a way to avoid disease, but as the choice of life itself.

It must be next to impossible for a teenager to think of us, most of us, most of the time, as people *at ease.* I doubt that the teenagers we care about would describe many of us, most of the adults they know, as fully in touch, in focus, in harmony with life itself. I would bet that we adults appear to live like greedy suckling pigs, attacking life without regard for balance, moderation, or consideration of one of life's most critical concepts: how much is enough.

As we strive to devour life, to beat it at its own game, we have become compulsive list makers. A majority of us compose daily lists, some mentally, some written out, others memorized, but all map out what we *must do today.* We become addicted to these lists to prove our worth, to prevent guilt, to occupy our time, to declare importance, to fend off anxiety, and to tell us and the world who we are. For many of us who are held captive to such lists, any mention of being stripped of them sets off a sense of panic deep inside. Without our lists, we feel empty; we feel desperate. We certainly are not at ease. We think we need the lists and accomplishments to prove our worth, that we are *doing* something.

For teenagers who think of adulthood as either an endless list of things to accomplish or a meaningless meandering with no destination, the choice is a catch-22. It should not be altogether surprising that a growing number of adolescents who think they face only those two choices are opting out completely. For them, suicide is a concrete way of expressing their rejection of such dismal alternatives.

It is time for us adults to ask ourselves if our lists and emphasis on "achievement by doing" encourage health, or are responsible for creating the climate for dis-ease. Here is a set of questions (another list, admittedly, but one designed to free, not bind) that might help us evaluate our lists and the fixation on *doing* that is their catalyst:

1. Who *really* wrote your lengthy list?
2. Who said you *must* do all these things?
3. *Why* must you?
4. If you ask, If I don't do it, who will?, have you ever let yourself *answer* that question?
5. To do everything on your list, how long would it *really* take?
6. Is your list written in pencil? Is it *flexible?* Does it allow for illness, or a bad day?
7. Is there anything on your list just *for you?*
8. Is there anything on your list just *for God?*
9. Is there anything on your list just *for fun?*
10. What would your list look like if *God wrote it for you?*

11. Is your list or God's list *tougher* to complete? Why?

12. Are there *rewards* for completing a list? What?

13. How might you be rewarded for *fulfilling God's list?*

14. Which list puts you *at ease,* your list, or God's list? How?

It is vital that today's teens learn early on how much lighter is the "yoke of Christ" than carrying our culture's burden to succeed. They must see us as serious about health, and wise enough to make choices that reflect balance and harmony, the hallmark of God's creation. I doubt if most of us, adolescents included, will ever stop writing lists, but we can at least compose lists that treat us fairly and graciously, ones that have room for *being* as well as *doing.* The smartest way to assure ourselves that our lists will be health focused, loving in their treatment of our own lives, is to surrender the pen or pencil to Christ. If Christ becomes the author of our lists, we will find ourselves *doing* less, and *being* more, not being burdened with obligations, but unburdened as we follow him.

The Balance Beam

Being healthy is like walking a balance beam. Keep your eyes ahead . . . slow . . . steady . . . feel the placement of your feet. Staring at your feet will make you lose your bearing. Rushing across will make you sway too much to the left or right. Trying too hard to do it right is a sure way to fall. Keeping your balance is easiest when you are relaxed.

Adults and teens need to keep their eyes fixed on God, and walk with God one day at a time. So often we pursue things, even health or holiness, with our eyes narrowly focused on the steps to be taken to quickly accomplish our goals. Teens with suicidal tendencies are notorious for trying too hard to keep everyone happy. Such adolescents are in danger of leaving the narrow way; they are headed for a fall.

But their lives, and ours, will stay balanced when Christ's yoke is accepted. He gives us rest, the contentment of simply *being*. His way of life means *health*.

BE
MATURE

*Grown up, and that is a terribly hard
thing to do. It is much easier to skip
it and go from one childhood to another.*   —F. Scott Fitzgerald

There is only one thing I find more painful to witness than my young son trying to win a friend by showing off, and that is an adult acting like a teenager. It is embarrassing to see so many of us acting as though we are addicted to adolescence, as though we will always be searching for our identity. We seem to be unwilling to face boundaries, borders, and other life limitations, and seem to be insatiable in our appetite for romance without genuine commitment. It is humiliating to see how so many of us try to avoid aging, and our real ages, as though they were plagues. Today's teenagers no doubt perceive that adulthood is an experience to skip, that it is much preferable to go from one childhood to another. If that is the message we convey, is it any wonder so many adolescents find the whole process of growing up not only distasteful, but, for some, frightening.

Although we all grow older and become grown-ups (at least in the eyes of our children), we do not all *mature*. Maturation is a choice, and like picking up our cross and following, it is a tough decision to make. It would be much easier to just skip it! Today's teenager (and today's world) is in dire need of adults courageous enough to make such a choice. *Maturity* must not be defined as becoming senior citizens, but rather as the capacity to handle the conflicts, crises, challenges, changes, and "crosses" of this life. We need a working definition of maturity, and an understanding of what is involved in choosing to *be mature.*

Maturity = Gratitude

Adolescents often ask these days about the wisdom of getting married. Lately I have chosen to share with them this story, not so much as a defense of the institution of marriage, but as a symbol of my gratitude for being married.

One morning around 3:00 A.M., having just conducted a wrestling match with my pillow, I was half awake and half asleep. The room was lit by the lime green aura of our digital clock, and my wife lay slumbering at my side. I decided to creep out of bed for something—a snack, a bit of TV, a little reading, a review of the newspapers from the past month, anything that might induce sleep. I tried all of the above, but my eyes remained wide open.

My back felt knotted, my neck as coiled as a serpent. Even my ankles ached. I felt doomed to greet the dawn unrested. I secretly plotted ways I might rouse Chris, but decided suffering alone was preferable to a violent death.

I thought a sneak peak at Justin might pass some time, so I slipped into his room. He looked up and said, "Way too early, Daddy, you go back to bed *this instant!*" I had used the same line often on him, and our trading of places caught us both by delightful surprise. I erupted into laughter and Justin jiggled with giggles.

Christine appeared at the door, grinning—fortunately. "What have we here?" she asked. Justin took the opportunity to tell of Daddy's arrival in *his* room, and of his instructions for me to return to my own quarters *this instant.* Chris's warm laughter melted my tension. We had a family hug, as we like to call it, a "love sandwich" with Justin as the filling.

Shortly thereafter, as my head hit the pillow, I knew sleep was only moments away. In those moments I felt my heart overflowing with thanksgiving. I felt proud of my little family . . . of being a husband . . . of being a father . . . of having a family hug at 3:00 A.M. I felt like a man, the sweet satisfaction that comes when I realize how good it feels to be a grown-up. Only as an adult, as a man who chooses to be a grown-up, could I experience the emotion that comes from gratitude. Maybe all real maturity begins with thanksgiving, and maybe all real sleep, of the blissful variety, is rooted in that childlike gratitude that prays each night so simply, "Thank you, God, for mommy and daddy and sister and brother and grandma and grandpa and aunt and uncle and teacher and neighbor and friends and my pet" and on and on. . . .

Maturity = Conviction

The young usher who showed us to our seats for what was to be a magnificent performance of the Broadway musical *Evita,* wore a punk rock hairstyle—pink forehead curl, straw yellow crewcut on top, the sides oily orange, and the wisp of a purple ponytail on his neck. In the plush reds and ornate gilding of the Performing Arts Center, and wearing a uniform fit for the center, not for the haircut, he was a spectacle. The more I told myself not to stare, the more his hair held my intense fascination.

A woman soon arrived at our row, draped in mink and wearing a sneer that cut like a switchblade. Our young usher asked to see her ticket, but she snapped, "Please get the manager. You are revolting. I don't pay good money to be ushered by the likes of you." After a brief but gracious exchange, marked by the usher's poise and genuine willingness to get the manager if that is what her ladyship required, the woman whirled, grabbed her program, and seated herself, two seats down from my wife and me. Separating us from her was an elderly woman, who reminded me of Helen Hayes, and her husband.

I spent almost the entire first act oblivious to the play, secretly thinking about what to say or do to the woman in mink. I felt guilty in my silence and passivity. Intermission gave me a respite from my plottings and presented at least the possibility of getting back into the play when it resumed.

As my wife and I sipped our petite glasses of orange juice, I saw the woman in mink joined by another woman, this one having done for the gold market what the other had for the mink producers. I then saw the Helen Hayes look-alike strut her way up to these two, plant her feet firmly in front of the mink matron and say quite audibly, "Your behavior to that young man was disgusting. He did his job, quite well I might add, and you are in no position to judge his appearance. It is August, and that mink looks absolutely ridiculous!" With that, "Helen" returned to her seat, leaving the women in stunned silence.

I could have kissed "Helen Hayes." She had the maturity to stand up for what she believed, to know her own convictions, and to refuse to tolerate what she found reprehensible. I did not know that lovely woman seated next to me in the theater, but I knew her ethics, her morals, her principles. It was pretty easy to guess what she stood for.

Does your teenager, or the adolescent or adolescents you care about, know what you stand for? Do they know what your convictions are? your ethical values? Could they describe your sense of morality, your principles, if they were asked?

There are many adults who own so much these days, who have accomplished such "great things," who have achieved fame and fortune, and yet who stand for so little. Again, maturity is a choice, a choice that mandates a clear awareness of one's convictions. Maturity as I am describing it is grounded in the ethics of the kingdom of God, and built upon a foundation of standing firm for one's beliefs. Our youth need adult role models who stand for something, whose lives reflect maturity and clear-cut standards and convictions.

Maturity = Service

There are few ministers who do not dread writing or delivering a stewardship sermon. In a stewardship sermon the minister talks about money, or as one member of a former congregation put it, "Is this the Sunday you ask us to fork it over in faith?" It is hard to get excited about preparing a sermon that seemingly, no matter what, makes the minister seem like a used car salesperson. No matter how much stress is placed on the offering of talent and time, most congregations believe money is the ulterior motive behind every stewardship sermon.

Stewardship *is* about money because money is our medium of exchange. A fact of modern ministry is that much of it requires ample funding. There is no possible way for minister or congregation to deny that serving people costs money, and *service* is at the core of most church budgets. If you ever peruse a sampling of church budgets, you will find a remarkable level of service indicated in each and every one. Meals and flowers and small seasonal gifts for the elderly; Sunday school and vacation Bible school and bell choirs for

children; counseling and marriage workshops and family seminars and spiritual retreats for adults of all ages; rafting trips
and pizza parties and horseback riding and discussion groups
for youth; Bible studies and prayer groups and worship and
music; support of all kinds to combat world hunger, to promote world peace, to advocate world justice; involvement in
hospices, Habitat for Humanity, respite ministry, meals-on-
wheels; the opening of doors to A.A., O.A., and other recovery
groups; day-care centers; nursery schools; and free blood-
pressure testing. The church budget is less a cause for embarrassment than a mature statement of Christian service.

It takes great maturity to talk rationally about money, even
more so within the context of a congregation with all its
diversity. A sign of the spiritual maturity of a church family is
whether or not every Sunday is stewardship Sunday, a call to
serve. The greater the level of maturity, the more significant
the service in scope and quality. Christian discipleship is
always costly, and in our modern world a major part of the
price is financial. Maturity and service are joined together,
just as the cross is inextricably connected to the resurrection.
What an invaluable lesson we can provide for our young
people simply by sharing with them the Christian service re-
flected in a church budget, a document that clearly displays
the challenge to *be mature* and to serve God.

Maturity = Courage

If we can, as adults, be honest about our fears, our credibility
in the eyes of adolescents will increase dramatically. When
we acknowledge our fears, we avoid numerous pitfalls that
traditionally obstruct adult and adolescent communication.
First, to admit fear amidst the terrors of this age simply serves
notice that we are sane. Second, the admission affirms our
humanness, which in turn removes us from the pedestal of

having all the answers. Third, admitting our fears shows we've learned to respond rationally to them, that we're not reacting to them in blind emotion. Fourth, the willingness as adults to share our fears invites adolescents to admit the fear that constitutes a considerable portion of their emotional makeup.

Often the adult tendency to act as if we have no fear signals to teens that we are, in fact, terribly afraid. To fail to acknowledge fear in a world that trembles daily is to come across as a fool, even a liar. It may be a winning strategy to avoid claims to real human fear in a political campaign, but it spells disaster in adult-to-teenager communication.

To accept one's fear but to move forward anyway is the final test of maturity and the essence of courage. To be mature requires courageous steps, the ability to make choices within a creative context of both fear and confidence. When we show our adolescents our willingness to stride confidently into the future, fully admitting our own trepidation, we have given them a much needed gift. We have not laid claim to the solution to life, to have the answer for all people or all situations, but we have carved out some answers for our needs at this time. A confident step, a single choice of courage, a mature decision made in a fearful atmosphere, provides a needed example of leadership for today's youth.

We do a great disservice to our young people when we put a happy face on every conflict, fail to address the most pressing issues of our day, and gloss over a crisis with simplistic slogans. Our youth look for leaders—mature, courageous adults who admit their fears, their flaws, their failings, yet who still are willing to march into hell for a heavenly cause. We have failed our youth miserably in this area, too often serving as cheerleaders for a future we say will be rosy and wonderful, while avoiding altogether the adolescent consternation over the much more basic issue of whether there will even be a tomorrow.

Suicidal teens tend to fail this test of maturity, being so afraid that they are, in a sense, scared to death. Until such time as these adolescents possess sufficient maturity to handle their fears, it becomes our responsibility as Christian adults to provide the courage necessary for their survival. If this means fighting some of their battles for them, so be it. If this means defending and protecting a spirit too fragile to defend itself, so be it. With suicidal youth we are always bargaining for time—time to breathe, time to gain strength, time to just survive. We must be courageous enough to do and be whatever it takes!

BE
HOPEFUL

*If it were not for hopes, the heart
would break.*
— *Thomas Fuller, M.D.*

Have you ever had the experience of knowing that something is missing, but you just can't put your finger on it? It
can be a haunting feeling, with the missing piece occupying
your mind like a chipped tooth attracting the tongue. Over
and over you trace the edges of the missing piece, trying to
discern what it was like when it was there; indeed, your only
certainty is that it was in fact present at some point.

I have been working with adolescents for twenty-two
years, fourteen of those as a minister, and have only recently
had the distinct impression that there often is just such a
missing piece in today's teenager. For the past two years in
particular, this missing piece has been the ghost at almost
every youth workshop, retreat, or recreational gathering I have
conducted or coordinated. With great relief, I found that missing piece as I contemplated this chapter.

The missing piece is *hope.* Today's teens are, from my personal and professional perspective, often without real hope. Though I still find most of the young people I work with to be bright, full of energy, basically kind, caring, occasionally crazy or rebellious, somewhat sophisticated, and on the whole normal, the missing piece for many of them is hope.

Many young people do not seem to possess a genuine belief in the potential for a better tomorrow, a conviction that life is basically good, or much confidence that they can even make a difference in life or in their future. Many adolescents have an empty place inside when it comes to real hope. They tend to fill themselves instead with grandiose materialistic fantasies, with hopes shaped by the desire for power and recognition, or mass media inspired dreams that conform to the standards of the world (Rom. 12:2). This absence of hope is a major catalyst for teenage suicide. If Thomas Fuller is correct, and the heart breaks without hope, then we have a good many adolescents dying of heartbreak.

As one young man said recently when I asked him of his hopes for the future, "Well, I know I want a Porsche, but I'm not so sure about kids." That may be a wish, but it does not qualify as a hope, at least not a *real hope.* Let me explain what I mean by a real hope by using a real life story.

What Is Real Hope?

Over the centuries, poets and philosophers and playwrights have thought the climate in hell would be fiery hot. They were all mistaken! At no time have I read the word *humid* in those descriptions. Dry heat I can handle, but heat coupled with high humidity would be eternal torture.

On one such hot and humid afternoon in the Midwest, I attempted to write a sermon at my desk, my arms sticking to the paper and the sweat dripping off my brow. I offered a silent prayer for the property committee, which had promised me an air conditioner two months before, and then decided I had two options: I could roll myself in "Shake and Bake" and roast here, or I could head for the lake. Getting into my car at first felt like entering a sauna with a plastic bag over my face, but soon the air-conditioner wafted cold air over me.

As I neared the beach I noticed a children's baseball game at a nearby park. Perfect! Watching the game would give me an excuse to enjoy the cool breezes off the lake without getting sandy or wet. I found a seat in the bleachers.

The crowd was made up of the usual fanatics that attend children's sporting events. There were fathers cheering their sons on to victory, and mothers yelling loud enough to rouse a hibernating bear. There was the mandatory couple (dressed for afternoon tea, not a ball game), whose son—the outstanding little carrot-topped pitcher on the miniature mound—was obviously the best player on the field, and who, together, constantly reminded all the other parents of that fact.

After watching the crowd, my attention was jerked back to the game by the awkward adolescent now at home plate. He was easily six feet tall, with hands and feet that couldn't quite remember what his mind had told them to do. He took three wild flailing swings at the ball and on the last pitch twisted himself into a pretzel and plopped to the dirt. The opposing team, out of respect for his height and due to parent-imposed politeness, held back their chuckles, as did his own teammates. He cursed and stamped his way back to the bench, taunting the red-haired pitcher who had easily struck him out.

I looked him over with pitying eyes. He wore a white shirt, plaid bermudas, black socks, and sandals. His boxer shorts rimmed the bermudas, and I knew every adult in the crowd either grieved for that man/boy, or tried to ignore him. But he, somehow both a victim and a bully, was impossible to ignore. It was apparent the other players had been told to overlook him, a destiny he was determined to prevent.

A few innings passed, and he was at the plate again. The first pitch: his windmill routine seemed mastered. Second pitch: pretzel time again. Third pitch: everyone knew immediately the pitch was way off course! The ball hit him in the head and snapped the blue batting helmet in half. In his first graceful movement, the boy slumped gently to the ground.

Everyone, including me, rushed to encircle the lump at home plate, the coach demanding air for his fallen player. I then noticed the faces around me and was deeply moved. The look was not empathy. It was not even compassion. For this grade school alien, the crowd had been transformed into a mass of mercy. Mercy—that divine desire to offer assistance and the embrace of grace. The crowd hugged that boy with forgiveness, forgiving even the barbs hurled at their own sons. The crowd wanted to take that boy, that awkward scarecrow child, into their arms and love him.

After a minute or two, he opened his eyes and leaped to his feet. Two coordinated movements in one afternoon! We all applauded as he dusted himself off and trotted to first. His first time on first! After the game he continued blindly to receive the aftereffects of mercy—everyone telling him they were thrilled he was OK and to be sure to have a doctor take a look at that swelling on his forehead. He told everyone he was used to having pitchers deck him, being a homerun threat and all. We all agreed. He lumbered toward his bike, yes, with a big wire basket in the front and a horn, and several boys told him, as he clumsily peddled off, that he could come over this weekend if he wanted. He grinned and yelled back, "Sure! I'll call you!"

Mercy forms the core of *real hope.* Mercy drags us out of ourselves. Mercy brings out the best in us. Mercy gives meaning, purpose, and value to the concept of hope. Mercy makes hope concrete, actualized, *real.*

As we left the ballpark that day, the hope in the air, in our collective souls, was tangible. We were, for that moment, filled with the power of being good, the optimism that always accompanies compassion, and the high spirits that flow from any act of human kindness. We had been transformed inwardly by a complete change of our minds and were basking in that knowledge (Rom. 12:1-2). We had become hope, *real hope.*

Real hope is never rooted in the egotistic self, and seldom comes from the action of one person alone. Real hope is grounded in the willingness to overcome self, to sacrifice our own wishes and desires, and to choose instead to meet the needs of another. Such choices, which create real hope, are most often inspired by a group of human beings who strive together to do what is pleasing to God. On that day the crowd at a ballgame, and the kids themselves, had become God's ambassadors.

In my many years of youth ministry, I have often witnessed hope actualized in young lives when adolescents have concrete opportunities to serve others. A haunted house for UNICEF, a Christmas carnival for cancer research, a Valentine's Day cookie bake for the sick and shut-in, a CROP walk, a canned-food scavenger hunt for Thanksgiving food baskets, a foster grandparent program, raking leaves, shoveling snow, or even cleaning an attic for someone unable to, somehow manages to lift teens out of the mundane worries of the day. Concerns such as how do I look? how do I sound? how do I come across? recede to the background. In offering service the adolescents stand on significantly higher ground where the view and their perspective are frequently more hopeful.

I have found, when ministering to a suicidal teen or an adolescent sinking in despair, that an opportunity to be an instrument of mercy is often enough to spark a flame of hope, including the desire to live and to love.

Are We Hopeful?

Too often our desire to help prevent adolescent suicide is matched in intensity only by our resistance to look first at our own lives. Still, though we cannot *do* much about teen suicide, we can examine ourselves, and determine if we are in fact *being* the kind of adults we hope our youth will become. In that spirit, we must scrutinize the status of hope in our own lives. Are we models of hope? Are we hopeful?

Strange as it may sound, when it comes to hope, we are often like black holes—burned out stars that have imploded rather than exploded. The fuel of our hope has been exhausted, depleted to the point that the gravitational pull of the negative aspects of life are so strong that our "light" is no longer visible. Stephen W. Hawkins in *A Brief History of Time* says that black holes aren't really black at all, but white hot. All that can be detected, though, is the gravitational energy of the blackness that enshrouds the imploded star. Carrying the analogy a bit further, I believe our hope still burns bright within us, yet the power of the negative aspects of our culture to devour our passion and compassion, the fuels of hope, is as formidable as the blackness of the burned out stars.

My strongest sense of this "black hole" spirit occurs when I counsel adults. The lives of those I counsel, as well as my own life, too often are crushed in the collision with our culture's standards of success. So many of us destroy our lives, our health, our souls, in a futile attempt to prove our worth to this world. Our culture appears capable of grasping almost anything other than the concept of *enough;* its measuring rod of worth remains the width of a pocketbook, and its chief value is the accumulation of things.

Since the whole system seems designed to leave most of us forever falling short, or feeling empty behind our shroud of designer things, it would appear to be a spiritual law of the universe that our hope is ripped apart upon entering this black hole of cultural conformity. Hope has a difficult time surviving in such a context.

Within these boundaries of culturally determined standards, I still find a miraculous capacity for hope, a white hot light of visions and dreams. At the center of our being the passion to live and love and learn still shines, as does the compassion that yearns to show mercy to another. Deep within us exists an eternal energy, a radical commitment to life itself, a burning desire to savor every moment of our lives, to celebrate with thanksgiving the hope that comes forth whenever we choose to be fully human, fully alive, completely God's.

In counseling—that grace-constructed framework of empathy, trust, and unconditional love—adults share the stuff of hope. In the privacy of the counseling relationship, adults often discuss those subjects adolescents desperately need to hear us talk about. Frequently with tears in our eyes and an ache in our hearts, we speak in counseling of our *longings.* What we *long for* is the fabric of our hope. What we *long for* we seldom admit to ourselves, to our God, to our youth. What we *long for* remains an inexhaustible supply of spiritual energy, an untapped source of real hope.

We must share these longings with our young people— the longing to skip in a rain shower, to play Hamlet, to be a poet or artist or philosopher, to discover a cure for cancer or the common cold, to wander through history, or roam the future frontiers of the universe. The eternal longing to understand, the instinctual longing to love, the secret longings of our hearts (to be needed, to be wanted, to be known) declare the true nature of our hope. We have failed to share with our youth the overwhelming "presence of an absence" (these longings) that they so clearly feel.

When we choose to acknowledge our own adult longings, those burning wishes of our hearts and minds, we reveal not only our hope, but our callings, the truth of who we are. In sharing these longings with adolescents, we do not simply inform them of our priorities, values, or special needs, but we uncover our souls so they might gain insight into why we choose life, why we find the whole enterprise of living to be decidedly worth the effort.

The more often we insist upon sharing these longings with ourselves, our God, our children, our youth, the more likely hope is to become a *habit.* By *doing* some behaviors repeatedly, even something as seemingly abstract as acknowledging our longings, we can acquire a habit that will transform our *being.* Prayer is something one *does,* but only when it becomes a habit does it become powerful enough to transform our whole *being.* If hope were to become a habit in our adult lives, I am confident that we would experience both a tangible rise in the level of hope within our youth, as well as a dramatic dip in the rate of teenage suicide.

What Do Our Longings Reveal?

It is almost impossible to speak of our longings for any length of time, to anyone we genuinely love, without feeling our eyes moisten and our inner core ache. Clearly, our longings reveal not only the depth of who we are, but also the ferocity with which we cling to these wishes of our heart of hearts. Our longings reveal a side of ourselves we cherish, we covet, we know to be as precious as a child.

When I hear adults reveal their secret longings, I am awed by the spiritual integrity of their wishes. Most adults speak of their wish to be a good Mom or Dad; to locate some meaning, purpose, truth; to experience real friendship, intimacy, covenant; to know the joy of surrender and pure service; to trust in prayer; to believe in God; to make a difference; to simply

enjoy one's life. Our longings often conform not to the standards of the world, but to the standards of Jesus Christ. Our
longings reveal a kingdom within us. Our longings reveal a
private wish, yet one generally shared by all humans, to become the children of God.

The vision of a kingdom where all tears are wiped away,
where mercy and justice reign, where all broken hearts are
healed with love, begins with the inner eye of our longings.
The kingdom, which is the expression of Christ's hope for our
world and our lives, takes shape out of the chaos of our own
human longings. The Spirit creates within our human spirit a
dream that is true, one that gives us the impetus to believe it
can happen.

In the Christmas hymn, "O Little Town of Bethlehem," we
sing the words, "O holy Child of Bethlehem, descend to us
we pray / Cast out our sin, and enter in, Be born in us today."
In our longings we see Christ born in us. In our longings Christ
reveals his hopes for us. In our longings Christ, the author of
all real hope, feels most at home, and we, at last, are at home
with God.

In our longings we also find a critical point of contact
with any suicidal teenager. Remember, a teen who seriously
questions the worth of existence is also a teen with longings
and with the need to know that he or she is neither crazy nor
alone. When we, as adults who care about these teens, express
our own longings, we not only relieve their fear that they are
cracking up, but more importantly, we open the door to the
possibility of real intimacy. It is this intimacy that is so potentially restorative to youth in emotional turmoil, and it can
only be offered by adults wise enough to celebrate the hope
that is in their longings. Shared longings mean shared inti-
macies, shared lives, life shared, which in turn always come
to mean renewed hope.

BE FAITHFUL

*It is as impossible for man to dem-
onstrate the existence of God as it
would be for even Sherlock Holmes
to demonstrate the existence of
Arthur Conan Doyle.*
           —Frederick Buechner

When I was a boy we used to visit this family I'll call the Taylors. I hated going to the Taylors. My sister hated going to the Taylors. My father loathed going to the Taylors. Even mother, whose childhood friendship with Vera Taylor necessitated these twice-yearly pilgrimages, found the experience pretty distasteful.

The car ride there was as cheerful as a trip to the dentist. I was silent in my rage at having my hair drowned in Brylcreem and parted like the San Andreas fault. My sister always sulked because she had to wear nylons and a slip. My father despised wearing ties on weekends, and when forced to somehow managed subliminally to convey to my mother that she was personally choking him to death. The only words ever spoken on the way to the Taylors were my mother's instructions on proper manners when in a "proper home."

The Taylor home was wall-to-wall proper. Every room was spotless, color coordinated, and arranged as though ready to be photographed for a magazine. Even their two boys, Harold and Walter, were always seated on our arrival, as though posed and awaiting the camera's click.

Mother always spoke of the Taylor home as her dream home, and for weeks following our visits she would comment on the glories of plastic covers that enabled the Taylor furniture to look brand new. Whenever possible, my sister and I conducted random searches of the Taylor closets, but were never able to locate the Taylor stash of plastic.

I thought the Taylor house was a nightmare. We simply could not move in the place. Our entire visit was spent in terror that we might break or spill something. We couldn't even go outside to play for fear of sweat. Everything happened in slow motion in that house; even my folks functioned like mechanical toys while visiting.

Dinner was always a disaster, even though my mother described it with words I never otherwise heard her use, words like *exquisite, gourmet,* and *heavenly.* The portions were miniature, and I hated eating without having milk to drink (dinner in the Taylor home was always accompanied with large crystal goblets of ice water). To this day, one of my strongest memories of our Taylor visitations is of being thirsty, since I never risked picking up that fragile, long-stemmed vessel.

After an afternoon of checkers and Monopoly, and a snack, my father's words, "Well, we'd better be going home, Hedy," were like the "Hallelujah Chorus" to my ears.

The ride home was so full of relief that even my mother's sighs and whispered words, "Wouldn't it be nice to have such a home?" went all but unnoticed. Home itself never looked better, all warm and worn, with furniture that looked lumpy and inviting. Most of all, the air was free of the smell of plastic, with the hint of Grimbol sweat like lilacs on a spring breeze.

Once, after returning from the Taylors, I told my mother just how much I preferred our home to theirs, and used as proof of my good taste the fact that every kid in the neighborhood thought of our house as home. Mother nodded with less than enthusiastic agreement, smiled slightly, and said, "Well, it sure is lived in."

The way Mom said "lived in" sounded sort of pathetic, but for me those words will always mean home. Lived in. Yes! Thank God! Lived in!

"Plastic-Protected" versus "Lived-In" Faith

Most adolescents are apt to think of faith as a visit to the Taylors. The faith they witness in our adult lives, or experience in our churches, is for the most part wall-to-wall proper. The only faith most teenagers have ever heard us claim is some doctrine-coordinated, dogmatically arranged formulation for keeping our souls spotless. This plastic-covered faith is often what our youth reject, since such a faith, like the Taylor home, appears unsuitable for human habitation. Adolescents, who by their very nature want some freedom and joy, instinctively sense that churches offering such a rigid, uptight, dogmatic faith will never feel like home. Like the Grimbols, they will flee such a suffocating atmosphere, tremendously relieved to breathe fresh air again.

If we are to be able to offer our youth the example and experience of a faith that is a home, a place where human beings can be fully alive, and not the Taylor tomb of checkers and Monopoly, we must fully comprehend the dramatic yet often subtle differences between a "plastic-protected" and a "lived-in" faith. Each of these faith models has its own style, spirit, feel, philosophy, perspective, and basic belief. The comparison following may offer some understanding of these faith styles, as well as insight into why adolescents can thrive within a "lived-in" faith.

Plastic-protected	Lived-in
1. Has all the right *answers.*	1. Has questions as well as some answers.
2. Proves the existence of God.	2. Experiences the existence of God.
3. Thinks God is a giant *no.*	3. Realizes God is a giant *yes.*
4. Says grace at the table.	4. Hears grace everywhere.
5. Never asks *why,* just has faith.	5. Asks *why* and watches faith grow.
6. Eliminates doubt.	6. Embraces doubt when it comes.
7. Always accepts the will of God as others define it.	7. Questions what the will of God is and seeks it.
8. Acts as though you know the will of God in most situations.	8. Feels the will of God at special moments.
9. Prays only at appropriate times and places.	9. Prays whenever, wherever, the Spirit moves.
10. Plays it safe.	10. *Plays.* Takes risks.
11. Worships without laughter.	11. Worships with laughter.
12. Loves ruts, rituals, and routines.	12. Loves change, creativity, and choice.
13. Tolerates children and endures teenagers.	13. Welcomes children and enjoys teenagers.
14. Celebrates Easter once a year.	14. Celebrates "easter" daily.
15. We are the same yesterday, today, and tomorrow.	15. Christ is the same yesterday, today, and tomorrow.

The Value of a "Lived-in" Faith

Adolescents simply cannot live with a plastic-protected faith. They cannot, at least most teenagers I have met or worked with, tolerate a faith that offers answers to questions they have never asked. They cannot handle adults who claim such certainty in their faith, as if their faith came with a guarantee, as if there is no room for question or doubt. Remember, adolescence is a period of life that instinctively requires endless questioning and the doubting of authority. If we are to accept adolescents as adolescents, and not expect them to act either as passively receptive children or sophisticated, conforming, pseudo-adults, we must embrace their world of uncertainty and testing of all supposed truth.

I happen to like teenagers. I also love the challenge of trying to inspire adolescent faith. I believe my enjoyment of teenagers is due to my acceptance of them as adolescents. (I have a terrible time with teens who act as though they have conquered life at sixteen, and an even worse time with adults who put these terribly "together" teens on pedestals.) I believe my ability to inspire adolescent faith is due primarily to my refusal to indoctrinate. I never offer a youth my own pre-packaged faith. I never remove from them either the pain of searching for their answers or the joy of discovering them.

One of the most positive, productive, pleasant ways to experience adolescents is to find the appropriate time and place to ask life's most consuming questions. Granted, the appropriate times and places are scattered and sparse, but they do crop up, and if they don't, once in awhile I take the risk of trying to create one, or even force one into existence.

Here are some of the faith-inspiring questions I have found fun and fascinating to share with teenagers, or better yet, small groups of teenagers. Before you say it, I will admit that *often* every question on this list is met with a look that says, "Who cares?" but there are other times when a question finds an open adolescent heart. The key is to never stop asking the questions, and to never give your own answer, even in the face of indifference—an adolescent art form.

1. What makes something beautiful? ugly?
2. What makes something good? evil?
3. Is war hell? Is peace heaven?
4. Why do we dream?
5. Why do we fall in love?
6. If Christ came today, what do you think would be the first thing he would do? Say?
7. Can a person choose to be sick? Well? to what extent?
8. What is truth?
9. What do colors teach us?
10. Are all people created equal?
11. Why do people pray? Worship?
12. How do you create hope?
13. How would you explain eternity?
14. How would Christ define success? Failure?
15. Why didn't Christ live to a nice old age, and die quietly in his sleep?

It has been my experience that adolescents only discover faith, or have it revealed to them, when they are encouraged to probe life's tricky questions. Adolescents can religiously tell us what we want to hear, parroting the truth according to adults and the church, but they only come to have faith in that truth, to believe in it, as well as *live* in it, when the quest, the questions, the answers, *the* answer, are *their own.*

What about Claiming Christ?

During my ministry to a congregation in Milwaukee, I worked with members of the social ministry committee to develop a visitation program for a nearby reform school for young men. The program's strategy was simple: our volunteers were to travel to the school one evening per week and bring humorous films, games to play, and goodies to eat. The purpose of our visits was to offer evenings of relaxed, homelike fun to a group living in an institutional, unfun setting.

For several weeks a dozen of us arrived loaded down with cupcakes and cookies, an assortment of electronic games, and Three Stooges movies—that ageless trio having proved to be a favorite. The young men knew nothing about us, except that we were lousy at pool, pretty miserable at ping pong, inept at most electronic games, but that we could match them in wolfing down cupcakes or laughing at Curly.

As we were leaving one night—it was our sixth week there—one young man asked, "Why do you come?" That one question enabled our group to share its faith in Jesus Christ. During that year we were able to witness to these young men in a relaxed and casual fashion, to let them know why we came, and why we saw the experience as anything but a waste of our time. Without preaching, lengthy discourses, or any kind of religious or intellectual explanation, we talked with these adolescents about our priorities, our values, our morals, and about making choices when one feels chosen by Christ. The young men came to know a good deal about Christ by their questions, and by our decision to live our answers.

Adolescents learn far more about faith from seeing faith make a genuine difference in the quality of our lives, as well as in the life-style choices we make, than by any creed or dogma or proof or defense we might offer them. When teen-agers see that an adult is happy, healthy, hopeful, and choosing to make a positive impact on this world, they stop and take notice. If we want to do something about adolescent suicide, *being faithful,* living as if Christ mattered, is a clear and convincing way of giving youths a reason to live. If we demonstrate that Christ has made a unique and powerful difference in our adult lives, a transforming difference in the choices we make as Christian adults, then we can expect many adolescents to choose such a life, a life which at its core is a radical affirmation of life as a whole. When faith is not something you *do* on Sunday, but something you must strive to *be* from moment to moment, it becomes *real.*

God does not die on the day when we cease to believe in a personal deity, but we die on the day when our lives cease to be illumined by the steady radiance, renewed daily, of a wonder, the source of which is beyond all reason. (Dag Hammerskjöld, *Markings*)

Adolescence can be a wild and turbulent ride, especially for those who find themselves in emotionally and spiritually "life-threatening" situations. Still, adolescence is also marked by a steady search for that which is genuine, a ceaseless quest for an authentic and livable faith. Suicidal teens, in particular, yearn for a faith that does not offer incredible answers to hardly credible questions, but one that will embrace the painful set of questions presently plaguing their souls.

Let us offer teens the model of such a faith. Let us offer them the example of a faith unafraid to pick up the cross of their very real, and very personal, agony. Let us offer them a faith we believe we can live, a faith we feel confident they, too, will find livable. Let us offer them a faith fully alive, a faith enmeshed in this life, a faith struggling adolescents will find available and feel capable of choosing in order to *be.*

BE
FAMILY

You don't choose your family. They
are God's gift to you as you are to
them.
    —*Archbishop Desmond Tutu*

Once, when I was twenty-five years old and still single, I drove back to Milwaukee after a midwinter break in Minneapolis with a few old college friends. When it began to snow I tucked myself in snugly behind a semitrailer. I followed it down the freeway for almost three hours, parasitically attached to the freedom of vision and movement it afforded me.

When the truck left the highway at the Wisconsin Dells exit, I started to cry. What caused this strange reaction? Was I afraid to drive through a snowstorm without my "leader?" No, that wasn't it. I had driven through hundreds of such storms, and knew another semi was literally seconds down the road. I was grieving! I had somehow momentarily, mysteriously become bonded to a truck and a silhouetted driver. I missed their company. I felt insecure. I felt the absence of any presence. I felt alone, anxious, and very much alien.

This strange event, as strange as most revelatory experiences are, made me aware of my loneliness. Though at that time I was successful and surrounded by a loving congregation, I still felt as if I had no roots, no sense of belonging, no niche where I fit, and no retreat of intimacy where I could find some spiritual rest. When I thought about how I wept over the departure of a semitrailer, I had to admit I was at a new ebb of insecurity.

That night I knew enough to drive on past Milwaukee to Racine, where my parents lived. I went home. I went to a place where I knew the smell, the sounds, and every worn spot on a rug, a step, or a piece of furniture. I went home to the weathered, warm faces of my Mom and Dad. I went home to be tucked in, as it were, under blankets of unconditional love, the love of my family. I slept soundly. My grief evaporated.

Many adolescents, especially those depressed or suicidal, feel just as lonely and lost, anxious and alienated, as I felt that snowy night on the freeway. Today's teens long to belong, to fit, to be known, to know, to feel the warmth that comes from a look of unconditional love. Our youth want to feel at home, to be part of a family, and they seek it with the same desperateness that drove me to Racine that winter night.

They Expect the Perfect Family

I have often heard parents, singly and as couples, complain that their teenagers expect perfect families, or have discovered such in the homes of their best friends. Most teenagers are well aware the "Brady Bunch" is dead, but often their parents continue to strive after some "Ozzie and Harriet" image. It is often their parents who repeatedly bring up the best friend's family as the model of collective perfection. It is often their parents who constantly try to shape the family into a trouble-free, idealistic model for all to emulate.

What today's teens need and want from family bears no resemblance whatsoever to a TV sit-com family, but is instead a family that celebrates the fact that they are a rare collection of human beings. In the following sampling of comments I've heard from adolescents, I hope you can see a rough sketch of their ideal family—a family not drawn with the perfect lines of a ruler, but with unencumbered, free-flowing lines. A family that shares real feelings and thoughts, and carves out mutual understanding, trust, and respect.

- "I wish my father could, just once, admit a mistake. It drives me crazy."
- "I wish my mother weren't such a martyr. I just wish she would only do things for us if she really wants to."
- "My father is always buying me something. The best gift he could give me is to love my Mom."
- "I wish my family could talk about sex, without my mother giving her half-hour seminar."
- "I wish my parents had friends."
- "I wish they wouldn't patronize me with all that phoney praise stuff. I just want the truth."
- "I wish my folks could admit my brother's drinking problem. It seems so absurd to ignore it."
- "After Grandpa died, nobody spoke about him for months. I felt ready to burst."
- "I want to fall on my face, and not have them rush in to pick me up."
- "I wish it was OK to disagree in our house. If you do, all hell breaks loose."
- "I try to tell them about my feelings, but they are always telling me what I feel before I can tell them."
- "I have a lot of doubts about faith and God and religion. If I tell them, they act as if I'm the right hand of Satan."

- "I broke up with my girlfriend. I loved her a lot. My Dad told me there were 'more fish in the sea.' I wanted to kill him."
- "I'm so sick of them blaming my friends for my behavior. Blame me."
- "Can they talk about anything except grades?"
- "I don't care what they say, complaining about my having a few beers while they hold Manhattans in their hands is a double standard."
- "I wish they just wouldn't compare me to my brother."
- "I like fishing with my Dad. Just sitting there quiet. Together. It's nice."
- "My Mom and I used to go for long walks. I wish we still did. We talked about the dumbest stuff. Now all we talk about is college, and drugs, and not getting pregnant."
- "When I'm home, I just don't want to even think about how I look, how I sound, how I come across. I just want it to be home. Where I can be me."
- "My father still holds a grudge against his brother for some stupid argument they had ten years ago. Then we go to church and listen to sermon after sermon on forgiveness. Why are we bothering to go?"
- "I sat on my parent's bed one night and talked almost until dawn. They just listened. I loved them so much for just letting me get it all out that way. I wish they knew how much it helped to feel as if they heard me."
- "They are constantly critiquing, evaluating, or interpreting me. I just want to have a normal discussion."
- "I don't want them as pals, but as parents. I expect rules, but I expect to be part of setting them."
- "If they want me to become an independent, responsible adult, they have to begin to treat me like one.

They have got to take that risk. Adulthood has got to begin someplace."

- "At the dinner table, when my Dad tells one of his stupid stories, well, sometimes we all laugh so hard. I never ever laugh like that anywhere else, until you can't breathe."
- "Mom makes Christmas magical, like some fairy-tale place. Every year I can't wait to see what she will create."

Our youth seek family life that doesn't hide the chaos, ignore the conflict, refrain from confrontation, or pretend to have intimacy. Laughter, tears, fights, forgiveness, independence, dependence, fear, courage, despair, hope, rage, grace, life, death, are all quite naturally woven together through a real family. That is what our youth want, and what they know they need, for only within the ups and downs of a real family can the creation of a warm, wonderful adult occur.

The Family as Lifeline

Remember the Chicago freeway maze my family confronted on the way to Elmira, New York? (See chapter 5.) Remember Mayor Daley's half dozen billboard greetings? Well, we did eventually make it to Elmira. Mrs. Hammond, my Dad's ex-landlady from typewriter school days, still puzzling over just when or how she had invited all of us, greeted us and worked furiously to be a welcoming host. A plump, pleasant lady of about seventy, her gentle smile revealed she often had to face the random winds of fate.

That first night's dinner, our family worked hard to be perfect guests, and Mrs. Hammond came to the table with a gift for me. I ripped it open with the feigned enthusiasm of a first Christmas present. It was a Zippy monkey doll. I was mortified. A fledgling jock, almost a teenager, I was virtually destroyed by anything that called my masculinity or maturity into question. Still, being the perpetual good boy, I did my parent's proud by dragging Zippy with me to every meal, and to bed every night, and offering Mrs. Hammond profuse, heart-felt thanks.

When we got home to Racine, Zippy promptly took his place in the rear cupboard in my bedroom. God forbid one of my friends should see me with a Zippy doll! I still am reluctant to admit this, but over the years I dragged Zippy out of his cupboard cave late at night when I felt sad, lonely, confused, or frightened. Clutching Zippy to my chest, some-how the pain or anxiety began to diminish. During lightning storms, before big tests, after major fights with friends, when a girl said no to my request for a date, when a girl said yes to my request for a date, even the night before I left for college, Zippy was tucked tightly under my chin.

Somehow, for adolescents, the family can be like that Zippy doll, an embarrassing gift teenagers want only to hide. Always a source of potential humiliation, the family remains something teens spend time with only behind closed doors, in private, preferably in the dark. For adolescents, family is a gift to be received publicly with joy, while quietly anticipating the first opportunity to get rid of it, but somehow knowing they will never choose to.

It goes without saying that every suicidal youth, every adolescent sufficiently depressed to question the value of going on, is in real need of something to give them comfort, some assistance more potent than a Zippy doll. The teenager trapped in an emotional and spiritual quicksand of anxiety and pain desperately needs support. The family that can be hugged at a moment's notice, offering the teen acceptance, affirmation, and warmth, usually enables a hurting adolescent to survive many a long, lonely night. Without saying a word, just being there, with a hug, a touch, a look, the family can serve as a lifeline for the teen whose condition is critical.

The family of birth or adoption, the youth group, the church—all can be that kind of family. That is our job! We may not feel that we get much out of the bargain, but I notice that my Zippy has some well-worn spots from being loved so long, so hard. So it is with families and others who may get a little worn-looking from all their loving and caring. But some things get better with time, and loving is one of them.